Nice 'N Easy

FAMILY
COOKBOOK

Cooking measures

DRY MEASURES

1 tablespoon	= ½ oz	= 15 g
2 tablespoons	= 1 oz	= 25 g
4 tablespoons	= ¼ cup	= 50 g
8 tablespoons	= ½ cup	= 100 g
16 tablespoons	= 1 cup (½ lb)	= 225 g
2 cups	= 1 lb	= 450 g
2¼ cups	= 1½ lb	= ½ kg

LIQUID MEASURE

1 tablespoon	= ½ oz	= 15 ml
2 tablespoons	= 1 fl oz	= 25 ml
4 tablespoons	= ¼ cup	= 50 ml
8 tablespoons	= ½ cup	= 100 ml
16 tablespoons	= 1 cup (8 fl oz)	= 225 ml
16 fl oz	= 2 cups (1 pint)	= 450 ml
20 fl oz	= 2½ cups	= 600 ml (1 pint)
32 fl oz	= 4 cups (1 quart)	= 1 liter
4 quarts	= 16 cups (1 gallon)	= 3¾ liters

EMERGENCY SUBSTITUTIONS

1 cup whole milk =
½ cup evaporated milk plus ½ cup cold water or ½ cup nonfat dry milk (reconstituted) plus 2½ teaspoons butter or margarine

1 cup sour milk or buttermilk =
1 tablespoon lemon juice or vinegar plus enough milk to make 1 cup, then let stand for 5 minutes

½ cup sour cream =
½ cup yogurt plus ½ teaspoon cornstarch

1 cup tomato juice =
½ cup tomato ketchup plus ½ cup water

1 square (1 ounce) unsweetened chocolate =
3 tablespoons regular cocoa (dry) plus 1 tablespoon butter or margarine

1 cake compressed yeast =
1 package or 2 teaspoons active dry yeast

1 tablespoon cornstarch =
2 tablespoons flour plus 4 teaspoons quick-cooking tapioca

½ cup dry bread crumbs (for coating food) =
½ cup well-crushed corn flakes

½ cup chopped nuts (for dessert topping) =
½ cup toasted rolled oats

1 tablespoon fresh snipped herbs =
1½ teaspoons dried herbs

1 small fresh onion =
1 tablespoon instant chopped onion, water added

Published by
H. S. STUTTMAN INC.
Westport, Connecticut 06889

© Marshall Cavendish Limited 1987

7P(1348)15-290

Library of Congress Cataloging in Publication Data
Main entry under title:

Nice 'N' Easy Family Cooking
Summary: A twenty-four volume, alphabetically-arranged cooking encyclopedia.

Includes index.

1. Cookery.

TX651.N52 1985 641.5 85-50818
ISBN 0-87475-433-X (set) 24 volumes

Cook's Notes

Handy hints and how to use them

Time
Timing explained including preparation in advance

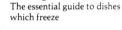
Freezing
The essential guide to dishes which freeze

Economy
Tips to make dishes go farther, or for inexpensive ingredients

Watchpoint
Look out for special advice on tricky methods

Did you know
Useful background to recipes or ingredients

Preparation
Tips for techniques, often with illustrations

Serving ideas
Suggestions for good accompaniments

Special occasions
Ideas to lift a dish out of the ordinary

Variations
How to liven up the basic dish

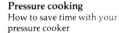
Cook's tips
Background information to help when you need it

Buying guide
Guide to selecting suitable ingredients

Pressure cooking
How to save time with your pressure cooker

For children
Adapting dishes for children's tastes

Storage
How to store and for how long

Microwave
How to cook the dish in your microwave oven

Nice 'N Easy
FAMILY
COOKBOOK

VOLUME
2
_____

BARBECUE
TO
BLACKBERRY
_____

H. S. STUTTMAN INC. PUBLISHERS • WESTPORT • CONNECTICUT 06889

Contents

Recipes

Appetizers — cold

Appetizers — hot

Main dishes

Vegetables

Salads

Suppers and Snacks

Desserts

Beverages

Barbecued Apricot Chicken

SERVES 4
12 chicken drumsticks, each
    weighing ¼lb, skinned
toasted almonds, to garnish

BARBECUE SAUCE
1 x 14 oz can apricot halves,
    drained
2 tablespoons vinegar
2 tablespoons light soy sauce
1 clove garlic, crushed (optional)
1-inch piece fresh ginger root,
    peeled and crushed
pinch of dried tarragon (optional)
salt and pepper, to taste

1 Prepare the barbecue grill.
2 To make the sauce, put the apricots and their syrup into the goblet of a blender, add the remaining sauce ingredients, season to taste and blend to a rough purée.
3 Turn the apricot mixture into a saucepan and bring to a boil. Boil, stirring, for 2-3 minutes until it thickens to a coating consistency.
4 When the coals are ready, lightly grease the grill and place drumsticks on it. Cook, turning and basting with the apricot sauce, until the drumsticks are coated through. The juices will run clear when the thickest part of the drumstick is pierced with the prong of a fork.
5 Transfer drumsticks to a serving platter and spoon over any remaining sauce. Garnish with the toasted almonds, and serve.

Cook's Notes

 TIME
Preparing and cooking take about 45 minutes.

 MICROWAVE
Omit step 1. In medium bowl, cook blended apricot mixture on High until thickened. Arrange drumsticks on rack. Brush with half apricot mixture. Cook on High until juices in thickest part run clear, turning once and brushing with rest of apricot mixture. Transfer to serving platter. Garnish as step 5.

VARIATIONS
Use ¾lb fresh apricots. Simmer the peeled, halved and pitted apricots with 1¼ cups water and ⅓ cup sugar for 10-15 minutes.

●300 calories per portion

Barbecued Chicken Drumsticks

SERVES 4
8 chicken drumsticks
¼ cup tomato catsup
2 tablespoons Worcestershire sauce
½ small onion, finely chopped
2 tablespoons light brown
    sugar
1 tablespoon lemon juice
celery salt
paprika
vegetable oil, for greasing

1 Combine the tomato catsup with the Worcestershire sauce, onion, sugar and lemon juice. Season to taste with celery salt and paprika. Brush the mixture over the drumsticks. Leave to marinate in a cool place for as long as possible (up to 8 hours, see Cook's Tips).
2 Prepare the barbecue.

Cook's Notes

TIME
Preparation 5 minutes, and up to 8 hours to marinate. Cooking takes 15-20 minutes in all.

VARIATIONS
Chinese-style spare ribs of pork can be cooked in the same way; so, too, can strips of belly of pork.

COOK'S TIPS
The flavor is improved if the drumsticks are left to marinate for several hours. The drumsticks can be skinned before marinating, if preferred, but the skin does help keep the flesh moist during cooking, and is extra nice if cooked until crisp. In the winter, the drumsticks can be cooked under a preheated medium broiler for about 15-20 minutes.

SERVING IDEAS
Serve with a green salad accompanied by chopped cucumber with yogurt and crusty French bread.

●275 calories per portion

3 When the coals are ready, lightly grease the barbecue grill. Remove the drumsticks from the marinade and place on the grill. Brush with the marinade occasionally and turn until the chicken is cooked through. The juices will run clear when the thickest part of the drumstick is pierced with the prong of a barbecue fork. Serve at once

Barbecued Corn on the Cob

SERVES 4
4 ears of corn (see Cook's Tip)
6 tablespoons butter, softened
4 tablespoons tomato catsup
½ teaspoon Worcestershire sauce
1-2 tablespoons finely snipped
chives

1 Prepare the barbecue.
2 Put the softened butter in a small bowl and using a fork, blend in the tomato catsup, Worcestershire sauce and snipped chives. Beat until well combined.
3 Remove the husks and silky threads from the corn cobs. Bring a large saucepan of unsalted water to a boil. Put in the ears of corn, bring back to a boil and cook for 6 minutes (see Microwave). Drain well.
4 Place each ear of corn on a piece of foil about 12-inches square, and spread with the butter mixture. Bring the edges of the foil together over each ear of corn and crimp them securely together, to make a tightly closed package.
5 When the coals are ready, place the foil packages on the grill and barbecue about 10 minutes, turning occasionally. Remove the corn from the foil and transfer to warmed serving plates with the buttery juices poured over.

Cook's Notes

TIME
20 minutes preparation, 20 minutes cooking.

MICROWAVE
Omit step 1. Place each ear on large piece of plastic wrap. Spread with butter mixture. Bring edges of wrap together to loosely wrap each ear. Cook on High until tender, rearranging once.

COOK'S TIP
When cob is out of season, you can use frozen ears of corn, which are available in most large supermarkets. Put the frozen ears in boiling water, bring back to a boil, then drain at once, place on the squares of aluminum foil and spread with the butter mixture. Cook for 20 minutes in an oven preheated to 400°.

WATCHPOINT
Never cook ears of corn in salted water because this toughens the kernels.

VARIATION
Use finely chopped parsley instead of finely snipped chives in the deviled butter mixture.

●235 calories per portion

Barbecued Ham and Peaches

SERVES 4
4 thickly-sliced pieces of ham,
   about ¼ lb.each
1 x 8¼ oz can peach slices, drained

SAUCE
¼ cup tomato catsup
2 teaspoons Worcestershire sauce
1 tablespoon vinegar
1 tablespoon light brown
   sugar
1 teaspoon vegetable oil
salt and pepper, to taste

GARNISH
parsley sprigs
8 stuffed Spanish olives

1 Prepare the barbecue.
2 To make the sauce, mix together the catsup, Worcestershire sauce, vinegar, sugar, oil and seasoning.
3 Cut 4 pieces of aluminum foil, each large enough to enclose a slice of ham and some peach slices. Spread some sauce on each piece of foil and top with a ham slice. Equally divide the peach slices between each ham slice, then top with the remaining sauce. Fold up the package and secure the edges so none of the sauce can leak out.
4 When the coals are ready, place the foil packages on the grill. Cook for about 10-12 minutes, per side, turning several times, until the ham is cooked through.
5 Transfer to a warmed serving platter and serve at once, with the cooking juices poured over. Garnish with parsley sprigs and olives.

Cook's Notes

TIME
Preparation and cooking take 20 minutes.

ECONOMY
Use the left-over strained peach juice in a fresh fruit salad or to make salad dressing.

BUYING GUIDE
Canned ham or thick slices of lean Canadian bacon can be used instead. If you use canned ham, you will only need to cook long enough to warm through.

●275 calories per portion

Barbecued Kabobs with Vegetables

SERVES 6

1 green and 1 red pepper, each
    seeded and cut into about
    12 squares
12 button onions
salt, to taste
12 button mushrooms
1 x 1 lb can pineapple chunks,
    drained
vegetable oil, for greasing

SAUCE

2 x 6 oz cartons plain yogurt
2 cloves garlic, crushed
2-inch piece of fresh ginger-root,
    peeled and grated
2 teaspoons garam masala or curry
    powder
juice of 1 lemon
pinch of salt

1 To make the sauce, put all the sauce ingredients in a bowl, mix well and leave to stand for 30 minutes in a cool place to allow the flavors to blend well.

2 Prepare the barbecue.

3 Meanwhile, to blanch the peppers and onions, bring a large pan of salted water to a boil, add the peppers and onions and boil for 1 minute. Drain and immediately plunge into cold water to prevent further cooking. Drain well again and pat dry with paper towels.

4 Divide the peppers, onions, mushrooms and pineapple pieces into 6 portions and thread them on to 6 oiled metal kabob skewers, alternating the shapes and colors as much as you possibly can.

5 When the coals are ready, place the skewers on the grill and brush with the sauce. Cook, brushing and turning, until the vegetables are evenly browned. Serve at once with spiced brown or white rice.

Cook's Notes

TIME
1 hour to prepare and cook the Kabobs from start to finish.

COOK'S TIP
The kabobs can be broiled. Preheat the broiler to medium and broil the kabobs for about 8 minutes, basting with the sauce.

VARIATION
Add rolled up bacon slices to each skewer.

DID YOU KNOW?
Garam masala is a mixture of Indian spices. Curry powder can be substituted.

●100 calories per portion

Barbecued Lamb with Parsley Butter

SERVES 4
1½ lb lean breast of lamb,
  boned and cut into 8 slices
sprig of fresh mint, or ½ teaspoon
  dried mint
1 small onion, quartered
2 celery stalks, sliced
salt and pepper, to taste

PARSLEY BUTTER
¼ cup butter, softened
½ teaspoon chopped fresh parsley
1 clove garlic, crushed (optional)
1 teaspoon all-purpose flour

1 Put the meat into a saucepan, add the mint, onion, celery and salt and pepper to taste, and just enough cold water to cover. Bring to a boil, skim off any fat that rises to the surface, then lower the heat, cover the pan well and simmer for 15 minutes (see Cook's Tips).

2 Meanwhile, to make the parsley butter, in a small bowl, combine the butter, parsley, garlic, if using, and flour. Season. Roll into 8 small balls, then flatten. Refrigerate while barbecuing the meat.

3 Prepare the barbecue.

4 When the coals are ready, drain the meat, discarding the flavoring vegetables. Then pat completely dry with paper towels.

5 Season the pieces of lamb on both sides, place on a piece of aluminum foil, then barbecue for 6 minutes on both sides, until well cooked and beginning to crisp.

6 Place 1 pat of parsley butter on top of each piece of lamb, then quickly transfer the lamb to a warmed serving dish. Serve at once, while the lamb is still very hot.

Barbecued Pineapple Steak

SERVES 4

4 pieces London broil or filet
   mignon, each weighing about
   ½ lb and cut about ¾-inch thick
2 tablespoons margarine or butter
1 small onion, finely chopped
1 cup tomato catsup
¼ cup lemon juice
2 tablespoons red wine vinegar
1 tablespoon Worcestershire sauce
2 tablespoons light brown
   sugar
1 teaspoon dry mustard
salt and pepper, to taste
⅔ cup unsweetened pineapple
   juice (see Buying Guide)
vegetable oil, for greasing

1 Melt the margarine in a saucepan, add the onion and cook gently for 5 minutes until soft and lightly colored (see Microwave).

2 Stir in the tomato catsup, lemon juice, vinegar, Worcestershire sauce, sugar, mustard and salt and pepper to taste. Bring to a boil, then lower the heat, cover and simmer for 20 minutes, stirring occasionally.

3 Remove the pan from the heat and stir in the pineapple juice.

4 Arrange the pieces of steak, in 1 layer, in a shallow glass dish. Pour the barbecue sauce over. Cover and marinate in the refrigerator overnight, turning once or twice.

5 Prepare the barbecue.

6 When the coals are ready, lightly grease the barbecue grill.

7 Lift the steaks out of the marinade with kitchen tongs and lay them on the grill. Reserve the marinade. Grill the steaks for 5-8 minutes on each side or until done to your liking.

8 Meanwhile, pour the marinade into a saucepan and heat through on the side of the grill. Brush the sauce over the steaks from time to time while they are cooking. Serve the steaks with the remaining sauce handed separately.

Cook's Notes

TIME
Preparation takes 30 minutes plus overnight marinating; 5-8 minutes cooking.

MICROWAVE
In a small casserole, cook onion and margarine, covered, on High until tender. Stir in catsup, lemon juice, vinegar, Worcestershire sauce, sugar, mustard and season to taste. Cook on High until boiling. Cover. Cook on Low for 15-20 minutes. Stir in pineapple juice.

BUYING GUIDE
Unprocessed pineapple juice has an enzyme that tenderizes meat, so do not use canned or bottled juice.

●555 calories per portion

Barbecued Treats

MAKES 8
1 small loaf of French bread
¼ cup butter
2 teaspoons country-Dijon mustard
1 tablespoon chopped fresh parsley
½ lb cooked chicken, sliced
¼ lb shredded blue cheese
2 tomatoes, sliced
8 stuffed Spanish olives, sliced

1 Prepare the barbecue.
2 Cut the loaf into 4 pieces, then slice each piece in half horizontally.
3 Beat the butter, mustard and parsley together until smooth, then spread on the bread. Arrange the chicken slices on top.
4 Sprinkle the shredded cheese over and arrange the tomato and stuffed olive slices on top.
5 Loosely wrap the bread slices individually or side-by-side in pairs in aluminum foil.
6 When the coals are ready, place the foil packages on the grill. Cook about 10 minutes, until the cheese is melted and bubbling.
7 Unwrap the packages, transfer to a serving plate and serve at once (see Serving Ideas).

Indian Skewered Lamb

SERVES 4

1½ lb lean lamb (preferably cut from the fillet or leg) cut into 1-inch cubes, trimmed of excess fat

2 x 6 oz cartons plain yogurt

1 onion, finely grated

1 teaspoon ground ginger

2 tablespoons garam masala or curry powder

½ teaspoon chili powder

salt, to taste

1 large green pepper, seeded and cut into 1-inch squares

1 large red pepper, seeded and cut into 1-inch squares

24 button mushrooms, stalks trimmed

vegetable oil, for greasing

1 In a large bowl, mix together the yogurt, onion, ginger, garam masala, chili powder and salt to taste. Add the lamb cubes to the mixture, turning them over so that each piece is well-coated with marinade. Cover with plastic wrap and leave to marinate in a cool place (not in the refrigerator) overnight.

2 Prepare the barbecue.

3 When the coals are ready, remove the lamb from the marinade but do not wipe off the yogurt coating. Thread the meat, the red and green peppers and mushrooms in turn onto 8 oiled kabob skewers.

4 Brush the barbecue grill with vegetable oil and place the skewers on it side-by-side (see Cook's Tip). Brush the meat with a little oil, then grill until the meat is tender, turning the skewers and brushing them with more oil every few minutes. Transfer the skewers to a bed of plain boiled rice and serve at once.

Cook's Notes

TIME
10 minutes initial preparation, overnight marinating. Preparation takes 30 minutes, then cooking.

MICROWAVE
Follow steps 1 and 3 using wooden skewers. Place skewers side by side on rack. Brush with marinade. Cook on Medium-high until lamb is tender, rearranging and turning several times.

COOK'S TIP
For those quantities you will need 10-inch metal skewers.

●365 calories per portion

Barley and Bacon Hotpot

SERVES 4
1½ cups pearl barley
½ lb bacon, finely chopped
2 tablespoons margarine or butter
2 large onions, thinly sliced
1½ cups thinly sliced carrots
1 cup chopped celery
2 cups thinly sliced mushrooms
2½ cups chicken broth
4 tablespoons chopped fresh
  parsley
salt and pepper, to taste

1 Preheat the oven to 350°.
2 Melt the margarine in a heatproof Dutch oven. Add the bacon and onions and cook very gently for 5 minutes, until the onions are soft and lightly colored.
3 Stir in the carrots, celery, mushrooms and pearl barley, then pour in the broth and bring to a boil. Add the parsley and seasoning to taste.
4 Cover the Dutch oven and cook in the oven for 1 hour, or until the barley is soft and nearly all the liquid absorbed. Serve hot.

Cook's Notes

TIME
Preparation and cooking takes 1½ hours.

FREEZING
Transfer to a rigid container, cool quickly, then seal, label and freeze for up to 2 months. To serve, thaw overnight in the refrigerator or for 5-6 hours at room temperature. Transfer to a Dutch oven, heat through until bubbling.

DID YOU KNOW
Barley was one of the first cereals discovered and was used to make bread before wheat. Pot barley is barley grain in its natural state with only the outer husk removed. Pearl barley is more refined as it has the outer layers of the grain removed as well as the husk.

●535 calories per portion

Barley and Leek Soup

SERVES 4
1/3 cup pearl barley
4 leeks, sliced
1 tablespoon vegetable oil
1 small onion, chopped
2 carrots, sliced
1 x 14 oz can tomatoes
1¼ cups vegetable broth or water
½ teaspoon Italian seasoning
1 bay leaf
salt and pepper, to taste
1 x 8 oz can lima beans, drained

CHEESY BREAD
4 round slices French bread,
   ¾-inch thick
3 tablespoons butter, for frying
1 clove garlic, cut in half (optional)
⅔ cup shredded Cheddar cheese

1 Heat the oil in a large saucepan, add the onion, leeks and carrots and cook gently for 3-4 minutes.

2 Add the tomatoes with their juice, the broth and the barley, herbs and bay leaf. Season to taste with salt and pepper. Bring to a boil, stirring, then lower the heat, cover and simmer for 50 minutes, stirring.

3 Meanwhile, to make the cheesy bread, melt the butter in a skillet until sizzling, then add the French bread slices. Cook over fairly high heat, turning once, until the bread is crisp and golden brown on both sides. Remove from the skillet, drain on paper towels and leave to cool.

4 Rub each side of crisp bread with the cut sides of the garlic, if using. Press the shredded cheese evenly onto the slices of bread. Preheat the broiler to high.

5 Remove the bay leaf from the soup, stir in the drained beans and heat through. Adjust the seasoning.

6 Toast the cheese-topped slices of bread until the cheese bubbles.

7 Ladle the soup into 4 warmed soup bowls and top each one with a slice of cheesy bread. Serve.

Cook's Notes

 TIME
Preparation takes 15 minutes, cooking takes about 1 hour.

MICROWAVE
In large casserole, combine onion, leeks and carrots. Cover. Cook on High until tender crisp. Add tomatoes with their juice, broth, barley, herbs and bay leaf. Season to taste. Cover. Cook on High until boiling. Cook on Medium until barley is tender, stirring two or three times.

 FREEZING
Cool the soup quickly after step 2, discard the bay leaf, then freeze in a rigid container for up to 3 months.

●340 calories per portion

Batter Puffs

SERVES 6
⅔ cup beer
1 cup all-purpose flour
2 tablespoons sugar
1 tablespoon butter, melted
2 eggs, separated
vegetable oil, for deep-frying
sugar, for dredging (optional)

1 Gently heat the beer in a saucepan until just warm (see Microwave).
2 Sift the flour into a bowl, then stir in the sugar. Make a well in the center. Add the beer, butter and egg yolks and beat together to make a smooth batter. Leave for 1 hour.
3 Preheat the oven to 275°. Pour enough oil into a deep-fat fryer to come one-third up the sides of the pan. Heat the oil slowly to 350-375°.
4 In a clean, dry bowl, beat the egg whites until standing in stiff peaks. Using a large metal spoon, fold egg whites into the batter.
5 Drop the batter, 1 spoonful at a time, into the hot oil, taking care not to overcrowd the pan. Deep-fry for about 4 minutes, turning once until puffed and golden. Remove the cooked puffs with a slotted spoon, drain on paper towels and keep warm in the oven. Continue in this way until all the batter is used.
6 Sprinkle with sugar and serve at once with cherry sauce.

Cook's Notes

TIME
Total preparation time (including standing, for batter) 1¾ hours.

SERVING IDEAS
Make cherry sauce while the batter is standing and reheat just before serving. Cook 2 cups pitted black cherries, with about ⅔ cup orange juice and sugar to taste, until tender. Then blend 1 tablespoon cornstarch with 2-3 tablespoons orange juice; stir into the fruit. Simmer, stirring, for 3 minutes, then serve.

MICROWAVE
In a medium bowl, cook beer on High until it is just warm.

●205 calories per portion

Fruit and Batter Bake

SERVES 4-6

1 x 8 oz can pineapple slices, drained and quartered
1 x 16 oz can apricot halves, drained
2 x 8 oz cans pitted red cherries, drained
⅓ cup seedless raisins
½ cup all-purpose flour
½ teaspoon ground apple pie spice
pinch of salt
¼ cup sugar
3 large eggs, slightly beaten
⅔ cup milk
⅔ cup light cream (see Economy)
extra sugar, for dredging
butter, for greasing

1 Preheat the oven to 350°. Butter a 5-cup heatproof dish which is about 2-inches deep. Mix the pineapple, apricots and cherries together, then spread over the bottom of the dish.

2 Put the raisins into a small saucepan and cover with cold water. Bring to a boil and boil for 1 minute (see Microwave), then drain and sprinkle over the fruits.

3 Sift the flour, spice and salt into a bowl. Stir in the sugar, then make a well in the center and add the eggs. Gradually beat the dry ingredients into the eggs and continue beating until smoothly blended. Beat in the milk and cream, a little at a time, making a thin batter.

4 Pour the batter over the fruits. Bake in the oven for 1-1¼ hours, until the batter is firm to the touch at the center, slightly puffed at the edges and golden brown all over.

5 Remove the pudding from the oven and cool for at least 15 minutes. Sift the extra sugar evenly over the top and serve warm straight from the dish (see Serving Ideas).

Cook's Notes

TIME
30 minutes preparation, 1-1¼ hours baking plus 15 minutes cooling.

SERVING IDEAS
Lightly whipped cream makes this pudding even more tempting.

ECONOMY
Make the batter with 1¼ cup milk or half-and-half.

MICROWAVE
Put raisins in a bowl and cover with water. Cook on High until boiling. Cook for one more minute.

●590 calories per portion

Sandwiches in Batter

MAKES 4 SANDWICHES
8 small bacon slices
2 tablespoons butter, softened
8 large, thin slices bread, crusts
   removed
2 bananas

BATTER
½ cup all-purpose flour
pinch of salt, to taste
2 large eggs, separated
¼ cup water
vegetable oil, for cooking

1 Preheat the broiler to high. Broil the bacon on both sides until crisp; then drain on paper towels.
2 While the bacon is broiling, butter the bread and then just before using mash the bananas well with a fork.
3 Spread the mashed banana over 4 slices of bread, dividing it equally between them. Cut the cooked bacon in half and arrange 4 halves on each banana-topped slice of bread. Top with the remaining bread slices and press down well.
4 To make the batter, sift the flour into a large bowl with the salt. Make a well in the center. Beat the egg yolks with the water and pour into the well, gradually drawing the flour into the liquid with a wooden spoon. When all the liquid is incorporated, beat well to make a smooth batter.
5 Beat the egg whites until stiff but not dry, then fold into the batter.
6 Dip the sandwiches into the batter, making sure that they are thoroughly and evenly coated.
7 Pour enough oil into a large skillet to cover the base and heat over moderate to high heat, until sizzling. Add the sandwiches and cook until crisp and golden on both sides, turning once with a spatula.
8 Drain the sandwiches on paper towels and serve at once.

Toad in the Hole

SERVES 4
1 lb large link sausages
2 tablespoons beef dripping or
shortening
1 tablespoon vegetable oil
2 onions, chopped
4 large tomatoes, peeled and
chopped
salt and pepper, to taste

BATTER
1½ cups all-purpose flour
1-2 teaspoons Italian seasoning
2 eggs, beaten
2 cups milk and water, mixed

1 Preheat the oven to 425°.
2 Prick the sausages with a fork and put them in a single layer in a wide baking dish or roasting pan. Add the dripping and bake for 5-10 minutes, turning the sausages occasionally to brown on all sides.

3 Meanwhile, to make the batter (see Cook's Tip), sift the flour into a large bowl and stir in the Italian seasoning to taste. Make a well in the center, add the beaten eggs and 2 tablespoons of the milk and water. Mix together, gradually drawing in the flour. Slowly pour in the remaining milk and water and beat the mixture into a smooth batter. Set aside.
4 Remove the sausages from the oven and drain on paper towels. Keep the oven at the same temperature for cooking the batter.
5 Heat the oil in a saucepan, add the onions and cook gently for 10 minutes, until soft but not browned. Add the chopped tomatoes, cover and cook very gently for about 5 minutes. Season well.
6 Spread the tomato and onion mixture over the base of a shallow ovenproof dish. Arrange the sausages on top and pour the batter evenly over them. Cook in the oven for 40-45 minutes, until the batter has risen and is brown and crisp at the edges. Serve hot, straight from the dish.

Cook's Notes

TIME
The batter will take about 10 minutes to make by hand, just a few seconds in a blender. The rest of the preparation and preliminary cooking take about 30 minutes. The oven cooking time is approximately 40 minutes.

COOK'S TIP
The quickest way to make batter is in a blender. Put the sifted flour, Italian seasoning, eggs and some of the milk and water into the goblet, blend for a few seconds. Add the rest of the milk and water and blend again until all the flour is incorporated and the mixture is smooth. Complete the recipe as steps 4-6.

●780 calories per portion

Bean and Apricot Salad

SERVES 4-6
1 lb fresh pole beans, thinly sliced diagonally, or frozen sliced green beans
½ cup dried apricots
1 teaspoon grated orange rind
salt, to taste
1 x 8¾ oz can whole kernel corn, drained
6 walnut halves, to garnish

DRESSING
1 tablespoon orange juice
1 tablespoon olive oil
1 teaspoon honey
pepper
few drops of lemon juice (optional)

1 Cover the apricots with cold water and leave to stand for 3 hours.
2 Place the apricots and the water in a saucepan and bring to a boil, then cover and simmer for 5-10 minutes, until the apricots are just soft. Drain, then cut each apricot lengthwise into 3 strips and mix with the orange rind in a salad bowl (see Microwave).
3 Bring a pan of salted water to a boil and add the beans. Simmer for 5 minutes, if fresh, or 2 minutes, if frozen, until the beans are tender but still crunchy.
4 Drain and rinse the beans in cold water and drain well again. Add to the apricots with the corn and mix.
5 To make the dressing, beat together the orange juice, olive oil, honey and seasoning to taste. Pour the dressing over the salad. Add a few drops of lemon juice, if wished.
6 Cover with plastic wrap and chill in the refrigerator for 30 minutes.
7 To serve, toss the salad again, and garnish with walnut halves.

Cook's Notes

TIME
Preparation 30 minutes plus 3 hours to soak apricots; 30 minutes chilling.

SERVING IDEAS
Serve with cold meats, such as pork or ham.

MICROWAVE
Place apricots and water in medium bowl. Cook on High until boiling. Cover. Cook on Medium until just soft. Drain. Cut each apricot into 3 strips. Mix with rind. In small casserole, cook beans and 3 tablespoons water, covered, on High until just tender.

●150 calories per portion

Bean and Avocado Salad

SERVES 4
½ lb shelled fresh or frozen lima
    beans (see Buying Guide and
    Cook's Tip)
salt, to taste
1 large avocado
4 tomatoes, thinly sliced

DRESSING
1 tablespoon wine vinegar
2 teaspoons water
1 teaspoon sugar
3 tablespoons vegetable oil
good pinch each of black pepper
    and dry mustard
1 teaspoon very finely chopped
    fresh mint or ½ teaspoon dried
    mint
1 teaspoon very finely chopped
    onion

1 Bring a saucepan of salted water to a boil and cook the fresh lima beans, for 15-20 minutes, until tender. If using frozen beans, cook according to the package directions. Drain well and leave to cool (see Cook's Tip).
2 To make the dressing, place all the ingredients in a screw-top jar and shake thoroughly, until they are well blended.
3 Halve, stone and peel the avocado. Cut the flesh into ½-inch dice and put into a bowl with the lima beans. Pour the dressing over and toss gently to mix.
4 Arrange the tomatoes in a border around a serving plate and pile the prepared salad in the center. Serve at once before avocado discolors.

Cook's Notes

TIME
Cooking the lima beans takes 15-20 minutes. Allow at least 30 minutes for cooling. Preparing the salad then takes 10 minutes.

BUYING GUIDE
Yield from beans can vary considerably but 3 lb lima beans in the pod should give you enough for this particular recipe.

COOK'S TIP
When using larger, older beans, remove their skins after cooking and cooling, to leave a bright green, tender bean.

MICROWAVE
In a medium casserole, combine beans and 2 tablespoons water. Cover. Cook on High until tender, stirring once. Drain and cool.

●285 calories per portion

Bean and Bacon Pie

SERVES 4
1 x 11 oz package pie crust sticks
2 tablespoons vegetable oil
1 large onion, sliced
½ lb Canadian bacon, cut into
 ½-inch cubes
1 x 16 oz can baked beans
1 teaspoon Italian seasoning
salt and pepper, to taste
3 tomatoes, peeled and sliced

1 Preheat the oven to 375°.
2 Roll out two-thirds of the dough on a floured surface and use to line a round 9-inch pie plate or heatproof bowl (see Cook's Tips). Roll out the rest to make a top for the pie. Refrigerate both the plate and top.

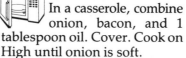

Cook's Notes

TIME
Preparation takes about 35 minutes. Cooking takes about 40 minutes.

MICROWAVE
In a casserole, combine onion, bacon, and 1 tablespoon oil. Cover. Cook on High until onion is soft.

COOK'S TIPS
Choose a shallow pie plate with sloping sides so that the pie filling will cook quickly and evenly.
 Pricking the top layer of dough allows the steam to escape during baking.

● 665 calories per portion

3 Heat the oil in a large skillet, add the onion and bacon and cook gently for 5 minutes, stirring, until the onion is soft (see Microwave). Remove from the heat. Add the baked beans and herbs to the pan, season and stir thoroughly. Spoon the mixture into the lined pie plate. Arrange sliced tomatoes over the top. Brush the edge of the dough with cold water and cover with the top layer.
4 Press the dough firmly around the edge, trim off any excess, then seal the edge and flute. Prick the top all over with a fork.
5 Bake in oven for 35-40 minutes, or until the pastry is golden. Serve with mushrooms and French fries.

Bean and Celery Soup

SERVES 4-6
1 lb frozen lima beans (see Variation)
4 celery stalks, chopped
5 cups chicken broth
1 teaspoon chopped fresh thyme or ½ teaspoon dried thyme
salt and pepper, to garnish
watercress sprigs, to garnish

1 Put the lima beans, celery, broth, thyme and salt and pepper to taste into a large saucepan and bring to a boil, stirring frequently. Skim any scum from the surface with a slotted spoon, reduce the heat to low and simmer very gently for about 1-1½ hours or until both the vegetables are very soft and thoroughly cooked (see Microwave).

2 Allow the soup to cool a little, then pass it through a strainer or purée it in an electric blender. Return to the rinsed-out pan and adjust seasoning, if necessary.

3 Reheat the soup gently, then pour into 4-6 warmed individual soup bowls. Garnish with a few small sprigs of watercress (see Special Occasion). Serve at once, piping hot.

Cook's Notes

TIME
Preparation time is 20 minutes. Cooking time is 1¼-1¾ hours.

VARIATION
Fresh lima beans can be used instead of frozen, when in season. About 3 lb lima beans in pods should give the correct weight for this recipe. Buy the beans when young and tender – once the pods have black patches they are past their best and are unpalatable – even in soup.

SPECIAL OCCASION
Swirl 1 tablespoon of heavy cream on the surface of each serving.

MICROWAVE
Put lima beans, celery, broth, thyme and seasoning in a large casserole. Cook on High until boiling. Skim off any scum with a slotted spoon. Cover. Cook on Medium until vegetables are very soft, stirring twice.

●60 calories per serving

Bean Feast

SERVES 4
2 x 1 lb cans red kidney
  beans, drained
2 tablespoons vegetable oil
1 onion, thinly sliced
1 clove garlic, crushed (optional)
4 tomatoes, peeled, seeded and
  chopped
salt and pepper, to taste
¼ lb thinly sliced cooked lean
  ham, chopped
1-2 tablespoons finely chopped
  fresh parsley, to garnish

SAUCE
1 tablespoon cornstarch
1 tablespoon soy sauce
1 tablespoon tomato paste
1 tablespoon light brown sugar
2 tablespoons vinegar
⅔ cup chicken broth

1 Heat the oil in a heavy-bottomed saucepan. Add the onion and garlic, if using, and cook gently for 3-4 minutes, until the onion is soft but not colored (see Microwave).
2 Meanwhile, to make the sauce, put the cornstarch into a small bowl, stir in the soy sauce, tomato paste, sugar and vinegar and blend to a smooth paste. Gradually stir in the chicken broth.
3 When the onion is cooked, stir the beans into the saucepan. Stir in the cornstarch mixture and bring to a boil, stirring until the sauce is thick and smooth. Simmer the beans for 10 minutes, stirring frequently to ensure that the sauce does not become too thick and sticky. Mix in the chopped tomatoes. Taste and season, if desired. Add the ham and mix to coat in the sauce.
4 Place the beans and sauce into a serving dish, sprinkle over the chopped parsley. Serve the dish either hot or cold with French bread and a tossed green salad.

Cook's Notes

TIME
Preparation and cooking take 30 minutes.

MICROWAVE
In a large casserole, cook onion, garlic and oil on High until soft, stirring once. Follow step 2. Stir beans and cornstarch mixture into onions. Cook on High until boiling, stirring occassionally. Cook on Medium-high for 5-10 minutes, stirring once.

VARIATIONS
Try other types of canned beans, such as fava or cannellini beans or soak and cook dried kidney beans, allowing ½ lb dry weight.

●300 calories per portion

Bean and Vegetable Soup

SERVES 4
½ lb Great Northern dried beans, soaked overnight and drained
1 tablespoon vegetable oil
1 large onion, chopped
2 slices bacon, chopped
2 leeks, chopped
3 celery stalks, chopped
2 carrots, sliced
2 cloves garlic, crushed (optional)
3 cups chicken broth
1 x 8 oz can tomatoes
1 teaspoon dried oregano
salt and pepper, to taste
2 tablespoons chopped fresh parsley, to garnish

1 Cover the beans with fresh hot water and boil for 10 minutes, then cover and simmer for about 2 hours, until tender. Drain.
2 Heat the oil in a large saucepan, add onion and bacon and cook for 2 minutes. Add the leeks, celery and carrots to pan with garlic, if using, and cook a further 2 minutes.

3 Add the broth and beans, together with the tomatoes and their juice, the oregano and salt and pepper to taste. Bring to a boil, then lower the heat, cover and simmer for 30 minutes until the vegetables are tender. Sprinkle with parsley. Serve.

Beat the Clock Beans

SERVES 3-4

2 × 8 oz cans baked beans in
  tomato sauce
about ⅓ cup instant mashed
  potato flakes, reconstituted with
  1¼ cups boiling water
1 tablespoon margarine or butter
salt and pepper, to taste
1 × 5½ oz can tuna, drained (see
  Buying Guide)
2 hard-boiled eggs, roughly
  chopped
2 tablespoons mayonnaise
1 teaspoon Worcestershire sauce
⅓ cup finely shredded Cheddar
  cheese
2 large slices bread, diced
2 tablespoons finely chopped fresh
  parsley
vegetable oil, for cooking

1 Preheat the broiler to high.
2 Pour the beans into a shallow baking dish and broil for 3-4 minutes, stirring frequently, until heated through.
3 Meanwhile, put the potato into a bowl, beat in the margarine and season to taste, with salt and pepper.
4 Flake the tuna into a bowl, then gently fold in the eggs, mayonnaise and Worcestershire sauce.
5 Using a spoon or a pastry bag fitted with a large star tip, pipe a border of potato on top of the baked beans. Pile the tuna mixture into the center of the dish and sprinkle over the shredded cheese.
6 Place under the broiler for 2-3 minutes, until heated through and the cheese is golden brown.
7 Meanwhile, heat the oil in a large skillet, add the diced bread and cook until crisp and golden.
8 Put the parsley in a bowl. Remove the bread from the skillet and toss in the parsley. Sprinkle on top of the cheese and broil for 1 minute. Serve.

Cook's Notes

TIME
This dish uses pantry ingredients and takes less than 30 minutes to make from start to finish.

BUYING GUIDE
Canned tuna is available packed in brine or oil; either may be used.

VARIATION
Increase the amount of tuna and omit the eggs.

SERVING IDEAS
Serve as an all-in-one dish or add a crisp green salad for extra color and contrast in texture.

●625 calories per portion

Herbed Beans with Eggs

SERVES 4

½ lb fresh or frozen sliced
   French-style green or snap beans
½ lb fresh or frozen lima beans
½ lb fresh or frozen peas
salt, to taste
4 large eggs, hard-boiled and
   quartered

SAUCE

2 tablespoons margarine or butter
¼ cup all-purpose flour
2 cups milk
2 tablespoons chopped fresh
   parsley
2 tablespoons chopped fresh
   tarragon or 1½ teaspoons dried
   tarragon
2 teaspoons lemon juice
pepper, to taste

1 Preheat the oven to 225°. Bring a large saucepan of salted water to a boil. Add the fresh or frozen vegeta-

Cook's Notes

TIME
If using fresh vegetables, preparation takes about 40 minutes.

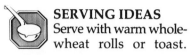

MICROWAVE
In medium casserole, combine vegetables and ¼ cup water. Cover. Cook on High until tender, stirring occasionally. Drain. Set aside. In small casserole, melt butter on High. Stir in flour, parsley, tarragon and milk. Cook on High until bubbly, stirring occasionally. Stir in lemon juice and seasoning to taste.

SERVING IDEAS
Serve with warm whole-wheat rolls or toast.

VARIATION
Zucchini, leeks, Brussels sprouts or cabbages can also be used.

● 310 calories per portion

bles and cook for 10-15 minutes, until just tender (see Microwave).
2 Meanwhile, to make the sauce, melt the margarine in a small saucepan, sprinkle in the flour and stir over low heat for 1-2 minutes, until straw-colored. Remove from the heat and gradually stir in the milk. Add the parsley and tarragon, return to the heat and simmer, stirring, until thickened and smooth.

Stir in the lemon juice, and season.
3 Drain the vegetables. Reserve one-third of the sauce and mix the rest into the vegetables. Heat through, very gently, transfer to a serving dish and keep warm.
4 Heat the remaining sauce in the same pan. When it is very hot but not boiling, arrange the eggs on the vegetables and drizzle the sauce over them. Serve at once.

Spring Bean Salad

SERVES 4
½ lb fresh lima beans
salt, to taste
½ lb frozen peas
2 avocados

DRESSING
6 tablespoons mayonnaise
finely grated rind and juice of 1
    small fresh lime
1 teaspoon sugar
pepper, to taste

TO GARNISH
Chinese cabbage leaves
¼ lb chopped walnuts

1 Bring a pan of salted water to a boil and cook the lima beans for 4 minutes, then add the peas, bring back to a boil and cook for a further 3-4 minutes, until the vegetables are just tender (see Microwave). Drain, rinse under cold running water to prevent further cooking, then drain again. Spread the beans and peas out on paper towels to cool.

2 To make the dressing, put the mayonnaise into a large bowl together with the lime rind and juice, sugar and salt and pepper to taste. Mix together well.

3 Halve the avocados, remove the seed and peel off the skins. Cut the avocado flesh into cubes and gently mix into the dressing together with the beans and peas. Taste and adjust seasoning, if necessary.

4 Arrange the lettuce leaves around a serving dish and spoon the mixed salad into the middle. Sprinkle with walnuts and serve at once.

Cook's Notes

TIME
This salad takes about 30 minutes to prepare.

MICROWAVE
In medium casserole, combine beans and 2 tablespoons water. Cover. Cook on High until very hot. Add peas. Cover. Cook on High until just tender.

WATCHPOINT
The salad is best served at once or the avocados may begin to discolor. Alternatively, peel and add them just before serving.

●440 calories per portion

Two~Bean Salad

SERVES 4
¼ lb dried red kidney beans,
   soaked overnight
¼ lb dried navy beans,
   soaked overnight
1 small onion, chopped
1 bay leaf
2 large celery stalks, thinly sliced
1 green pepper, seeded and diced

DRESSING
6 tablespoons olive oil
2 tablespoons wine vinegar
1 clove garlic, crushed
   (optional)
salt and pepper, to taste

1 Drain the kidney beans, transfer to a saucepan, cover with water and bring to a boil. Boil vigorously for 10 minutes, then add the navy beans, together with their soaking liquid. Add the onion and bay leaf and bring back to a boil. Reduce the heat, half cover with a lid and simmer for about 1 hour, until tender.

2 Meanwhile, to make the dressing, put the ingredients in a screw-top jar with seasoning to taste. Replace the lid firmly and shake well to mix.

3 Drain the beans and discard the cooking liquid and bay leaf. Transfer to a serving dish and pour the dressing over, while the beans are still warm (see Cook's Tip). Mix well and leave to stand for at least 1 hour.

4 Add the celery and diced pepper to the beans, taste and adjust seasoning and mix well. Serve.

Cook's Notes

TIME
10 minutes preparation, then 1¼ hours cooking and at least 1 hour standing time.

WATCHPOINT
The kidney beans must be boiled vigorously before simmering, to remove poisonous elements.

COOK'S TIP
The beans will absorb more flavor if they are still warm when dressed.

● 330 calories per portion

Chinese Bean Sprout Salad

SERVES 4
½ lb bean sprouts
½ large cucumber, peeled
⅛ lb collard greens, stems
    removed and finely shredded
⅓ cup roasted peanuts
salt and pepper, to taste

DRESSING
⅓ cup crumbled Danish Blue
    cheese
6 tablespoons vegetable oil
2 tablespoons wine vinegar
a little milk (optional)

Cook's Notes

TIME
Preparation takes about 20 minutes.

SERVING IDEAS
Serve as a side dish with beef casseroles, hot roast lamb or broiled white fish as an appetizer.

COOK'S TIP
If you have a blender or food processor, put all the dressing ingredients in the machine together and work until smooth.

SPECIAL OCCASION
If you are feeling extravagant, for a dinner party or special occasion, try using Roquefort, which is a fine French blue cheese, available from delicatessens and good supermarkets.

WATCHPOINT
Add the peanuts just before you dress the salad, so that they do not lose their crunchiness.

• 345 calories per portion

1 Cut the cucumber into 1½-inch pieces, then cut these lengthwise into thin sticks. Place in a salad bowl with the bean sprouts.
2 Add the collard greens and mix all the vegetables together.
3 To make the dressing, place the blue cheese into a bowl and mash with a fork. Add the oil a little at a time, mixing it into the cheese with the fork to form a paste. Mix in the vinegar and add a little milk if the mixture seems too thick for a dressing (see Cook's Tip).

4 Just before serving, add the peanuts to the salad and pour the dressing over. Toss until all the ingredients are thoroughly coated in the dressing, then add salt and pepper to taste. Serve at once while the bean sprouts and nuts are crunchy.

Chinese-Style Chicken

SERVES 4

½ lb fresh bean sprouts (see
   Variation)
4 cups cubed, skinned, cooked
   chicken (see Cook's Tip)
3 tablespoons vegetable oil
1½ teaspoons cornstarch
1 tablespoon water
⅔ cup chicken broth
1 large onion, thinly sliced
2 carrots, coarsely grated
1 small green pepper, seeded and
   finely diced
1 clove garlic, crushed (optional)
1-inch piece fresh ginger root,
   finely chopped
1 tablespoon dry sherry
2 tablespoons soy sauce
salt and pepper, to taste

1 Heat 2 tablespoons of the oil in a
large skillet or wok, add the bean
sprouts and cook briskly for 1
minute, stirring all the time.
2 Remove the bean sprouts with a
slotted spoon and set aside. In a
pitcher or measuring cup, blend the
cornstarch with the water to make a
smooth paste. Stir in the broth.
3 Heat the remaining oil in the skillet or wok, add the chicken, onion,
carrots, green pepper, garlic, if
using, and fresh ginger root and stir-
fry for 2-3 minutes.
4 Stir the thickened broth into the
skillet or wok, together with the
sherry and soy sauce. Stir well to
mix. Bring to a boil, stirring, and
cook for 2 minutes. Taste and adjust
the seasoning.
5 Return the bean sprouts to the pan
and heat through gently, stirring.
6 Pile the mixture into a warmed
serving dish, or serve straight from
the wok, if using. Serve at once.

Cook's Notes

TIME
Preparation 15 minutes,
cooking 10 minutes.

COOK'S TIP
This quick-to-prepare
dish is an excellent
way of making a hot, tasty
meal with ready-cooked chicken pieces from supermarkets.
Three cooked chicken breasts
should give enough meat for 4
people as here.

VARIATION
If fresh bean sprouts
are not available, use
canned. Drain and omit initial
cooking in step 1.

●240 calories per portion

Oriental Steak Salad

SERVES 4
⅓ lb bean sprouts
½ lb London broil or filet mignon
salt, to taste
½ cup long grain rice
⅔ cup frozen peas
1 large carrot, grated
1 teaspoon ground ginger
pepper
½ cup sliced button mushrooms

MARINADE
¼ cup dry red wine
2 tablespoons soy sauce
1 tablespoon lemon juice
1-inch piece ginger root,
   peeled and grated
2 teaspoons soft dark brown sugar

TO GARNISH
lettuce leaves
¼ cup slivered almonds
cucumber slices

1 Bring a saucepan of salted water to a boil and cook the long grain rice for about 12 minutes, until just tender. Drain and rinse under cold running water for 1 minute. Drain again.
2 Cook the peas according to package directions, then drain and rinse under cold running water. Mix the rice, peas and grated carrot together in a bowl. Cover and refrigerate.
3 Preheat the broiler to very high. Rub the ground ginger evenly over both sides of the steak, seasoning to taste. Broil for 5-7 minutes on either side, then leave to cool slightly.
4 Mix the marinade ingredients in a jar with ½ teaspoon salt, or to taste.
5 Slice the steak into very thin strips, then put in a bowl and pour over the marinade. Stir the meat to make sure it is thoroughly coated, then leave in a cool place for 3-4 hours, stirring occasionally.
6 When ready to serve, remove the steak with a slotted spoon and reserve the marinade. Stir the meat, the bean sprouts and the mushrooms into the rice mixture. Add 2 tablespoons of the marinade and gently stir to combine well.
7 To serve, arrange the lettuce leaves in a salad bowl, pile the salad in the center then sprinkle the almonds over and garnish with cucumber slices.

Cook's Notes

TIME
The salad takes about 20 minutes to prepare but, for best results, the steak should marinate for 3-4 hours after it has been cooked.

SERVING IDEAS
This makes a tasty light lunch on its own.

BUYING GUIDE
Although London broil or filet mignon are expensive, very little is needed for this dish.

●260 calories per portion

Stir~Fried Bean Sprouts

SERVES 4
½ lb bean sprouts
1 cup sliced mushrooms (see
    Buying Guide)
½ lb small French-style beans
    left whole (see Buying Guide)
2 tablespoons vegetable oil
1 onion, sliced
¼ cup water
1 tablespoon light soy sauce
1 tablespoon lemon juice
salt and pepper, to taste.

1 Heat the oil in a wok or large heavy-bottomed saucepan. Cook the onion for 2 minutes, then add the beans and stir-fry for 1 minute.
2 Add the water, soy sauce, lemon juice and season to taste. Cook for 5 minutes, tossing the beans in the liquid until it has evaporated.
3 Add the mushrooms and stir constantly, until they are tender. Add bean sprouts and stir-fry for a further 2 minutes until the bean sprouts are heated through and just tender, but still crisp. Transfer to a warmed serving dish and serve at once with roasted or broiled meat.

Cook's Notes

TIME
Preparation time is 5 minutes and cooking time about 10 minutes.

BUYING GUIDE
Small, thin French-style green beans are best for stir-frying and they will give the crunchiest result.
Choose button mushrooms for this recipe – they make an attractive addition and will give the dish a lighter color.

●85 calories per portion

Beef with Creamy Wine Sauce

SERVES 4
2 lb rolled boneless rump
3 tablespoons shortening
2 cups sliced carrots
2 cups sliced leeks
1 onion, quartered
8 cloves
⅔ cup red wine
¼ cup sour cream
¼ teaspoon ground apple pie
   spice
salt and pepper, to taste

1 Preheat the oven to 325°.
2 Melt the shortening over medium heat in a Dutch oven large enough to hold the vegetables and the beef. When the shortening is smoking, add the beef and turn to brown on all sides. Remove the beef from the pan and set aside. Pour away all but 2 tablespoons of the fat in the pan.
3 Add the carrots and leeks to the Dutch oven and mix, gently stirring to coat the vegetables evenly with the hot fat.
4 Put the browned beef on top of the vegetables. Stick 2 cloves into each onion quarter and arrange them around the beef.
5 Add the red wine and water to the pan and bring to a boil. Transfer to the oven and cook for 1½ hours, turning the meat once.
6 Remove the beef, discard the string and carve into slices. Remove the vegetables with a slotted spoon and put them on a warmed serving dish. Arrange the sliced beef on top. Keep hot in the oven at the lowest possible temperature.
7 Rapidly boil the cooking liquid in the Dutch oven for about 5 minutes, until reduced slightly. Remove from the heat and stir in the sour cream and spices. Season to taste. Heat through very gently, but do not allow to boil. Pour a little of the sauce over the beef, then serve at once, with the remaining sauce handed separately in a warmed pitcher.

Cook's Notes

TIME
Preparation takes about 10 minutes. Cooking takes about 1¾ hours.

COOK'S TIP
The sauce is quite thin. If you prefer a thicker sauce, thicken it either with 2 teaspoons cornstarch blended with a little water, or with 1 tablespoon butter mixed to a paste with 1 tablespoon all-purpose flour. Either mixture should be added to the sauce before the cream. Add a little hot sauce to the blended cornstarch, then stir into the sauce and let it boil for a minute or two. Beat in the butter and flour paste a little at a time while the sauce is boiling.

VARIATIONS
Use any root vegetables that are in season.

SERVING IDEAS
All that is needed to accompany the meat and vegetables is mashed potatoes, to soak up the sauce. Alternatively, serve the dish with hot, crusty French bread.

●565 calories per portion

Beef and Eggplant Braise

SERVES 4
2 lb beef round rump roast, rolled and tied (see Buying Guide)
1½ lb eggplant, cut into ¾-inch cubes
salt, to taste
3 tablespoons vegetable oil
3 onions, chopped
1 clove garlic, crushed
1 carrot, thinly sliced
1 x 14 oz can chopped tomatoes
pepper

1 Put the eggplant cubes into a colander, sprinkle with salt, put a plate on top and weight down. Leave to drain for about 30 minutes to remove the bitter juices.
2 Dry the beef with paper towels.

Heat the oil in a large, heavy-bottomed Dutch oven or saucepan. Add beef and cook 2-3 minutes, turning meat once or twice, to brown on all sides. Drain the beef over the pan and set aside on a plate.
3 Add the onions and garlic to the pan and cook gently for 5 minutes until soft and lightly colored. Add the carrot, stir well and cook for a further 1 minute.
4 Rinse the eggplant under cold running water, pat dry and add to the pan. Add the chopped tomatoes with their juice, season and stir well. Return the beef to the pan and cover tightly. Cook very gently for about 2½ hours or until the beef is cooked to your liking.
5 Transfer the beef to a warmed serving dish. Taste the vegetables and adjust seasoning if necessary. Carve the beef into neat slices and spoon the vegetables around it. Serve at once.

Brisket and Carrots

SERVES 6
3-3½ lb corned beef brisket
1 bay leaf
6 whole black peppercorns
1 onion, quartered
1½ lb carrots, quartered

PARSLEY SAUCE
2 tablespoons margarine or butter
¼ cup all-purpose flour
⅔ cup milk
2 tablespoons finely chopped fresh
     parsley
salt and pepper, to taste

1 Put the brisket in a very large saucepan with the bay leaf, peppercorns and onion. Cover with cold water and bring slowly to a boil, skimming off any fat as it rises to the surface. Cover and simmer gently for 1½ hours.
2 Add the carrots to the pan, cover again and simmer for a further 30 minutes or until the carrots are just cooked and the brisket is tender and flakes slightly when pierced with the point of a sharp knife.
3 Preheat the oven to 225°.
4 Carve the beef and place on a large warmed dish and, with a slotted spoon, arrange the carrots around it. Keep warm in the oven. Using paper towels, blot off surface fat from the pan and reserve the broth for making the parsley sauce.
5 To make the parsley sauce, melt the margarine in a small saucepan. Sprinkle in the flour and stir over low heat for 1-2 minutes, until straw-colored. Remove from the heat and gradually stir in ⅔ cup of the reserved broth and the milk. Return to the heat and simmer, stirring, until thick and smooth. Stir in three-quarters of the parsley and season to taste with salt and pepper.
6 Remove the boiled brisket and the carrots from the oven and serve at once. Hand the sauce separately in a warmed jug. Sprinkle with the remaining parsley before serving.

Cook's Notes

TIME
Preparation takes 15-20 minutes. Cooking takes about 2½ hours.

DID YOU KNOW
Boiled beef and carrots is a traditional English cold-weather dish. Particularly popular with Londoners, it is celebrated in the Cockney song of the same title.

SERVING IDEAS
Serve with lightly boiled cabbage and boiled or mashed potatoes, accompanied by English mustard or horseradish sauce.

COOK'S TIP
Always use fresh parsley for this sauce.

●430 calories per portion

Brisket with Green Sauce

SERVES 4
2-2¼ lb brisket of beef
(see Buying Guide)
2 carrots, cut into chunks
1 small onion, chopped
salt and pepper, to taste

SAUCE
2 tablespoons capers, rinsed and
finely chopped
1 clove garlic, crushed (optional)
½ small onion, very finely chopped
¼ cup finely chopped fresh parsley
juice of ½ lemon
4 anchovy fillets, very finely
chopped
⅔ cup vegetable oil

1 Weigh the brisket and calculate the cooking time: allow 25 minutes to each 1 lb plus a further 25 minutes.
2 Place the brisket in a large saucepan with the carrots and onion and salt and pepper to taste. Cover with fresh cold water, gradually bring to a boil, then lower the heat, cover the pan, and simmer for the calculated cooking time, until cooked through (the juices should run clear when the meat is pierced with a sharp knife).
3 Meanwhile, to make the sauce, place all the sauce ingredients, except the oil, in a blender and blend for a few seconds. Very gradually pour in the oil, with the motor running, stopping to scrape down the sides if necessary. Blend until the capers, parsley and anchovies are fine and the sauce is smooth. Season to taste with salt and pepper (see Cook's Tip for alternative method).
4 Remove the cooked brisket from the pan and leave to cool slightly, discarding the cooking vegetables, but keeping the liquid for broth. Remove the string, then transfer the beef to a warmed serving dish. Carve a few medium-thick slices of the brisket and spoon over a little of the sauce. Hand the remaining green sauce separately.

Cook's Notes

TIME
Preparation takes about 10 minutes. Cooking about 1¼ hours. Make the sauce while the meat cooks.

COOK'S TIP
If you do not have a blender or food processor, put all the sauce ingredients, except the oil, in a bowl. Beating with a fork, very gradually add the oil until evenly blended, then season to taste with salt and pepper.

SERVING IDEAS
Serve the brisket hot with plain boiled potatoes and another root vegetable such as diced rutabagas. The brisket is also delicious served cold.

BUYING GUIDE
Brisket of beef is lean, coarse-grained meat which benefits from long, slow cooking to tenderize it.

●585 calories per portion

Beef in Stout

SERVES 4-6

2½-3½ lb bottom round of beef
1¼ cups stout (see Economy and
   Did You Know)
¼ cup vegetable oil
2 large onions, sliced
1 tablespoon all-purpose flour
1 teaspoon Italian seasoning
salt and pepper, to taste
¼ cup tomato paste
watercress and mushrooms (see
   Preparation), to garnish

1 Place the meat in a bowl and pour the stout over. Cover and leave to marinate for 2 hours, turning the meat occasionally.

2 Preheat the oven to 325°. Remove the beef from the marinade, and pat dry with paper towels. Reserve the stout marinade.

3 Heat 2 tablespoons of the oil in a heatproof Dutch oven, add the beef and brown on all sides over high heat. Remove from the pan and reserve in a warm place.

4 Heat the remaining oil in the Dutch oven, add the onions and cook over low heat until soft and lightly colored. Sprinkle in the flour, stir for 2 minutes, then stir in the reserved marinade and bring to a boil. Add the herbs and season to taste.

5 Return the beef to the Dutch oven, cover and cook for 2½ hours, until tender. Transfer the meat to a warmed serving dish and keep warm.

6 Place the casserole on top of the stove and remove any fat from the liquid by blotting the surface with paper towels. Stir in the tomato paste and bring to a boil. Simmer for 5 minutes to thicken slightly, then taste and adjust seasoning.

7 Carve a few slices of the beef, then pour a little of the sauce over the top. Garnish with watercress and mushrooms and serve at once, with remaining sauce handed separately in a warmed pitcher.

Cook's Notes

 TIME
Preparation time is 20 minutes, but allow 2 hours for the meat to marinate. Cooking time is 2½ hours.

DID YOU KNOW
Stout is a strong dark beer brewed with roasted malt or barley from England. It is available in liquor stores specializing in international drinks. The acid content in stout helps break down the tough fibers and connective tissues in meat.

PREPARATION
To flute mushrooms, make shallow curved cuts in the cap, turning the mushroom as you work.

ECONOMY
You can substitute beef broth for the stout.

●695 calories per portion

Chili Pot Roast

SERVES 4

2½ lb brisket of beef,
   boned, rolled and tied
1 tablespoon vegetable oil
2 tablespoons margarine or butter
2 large onions, sliced
2 cloves garlic, crushed
   (optional)
2 carrots, sliced
2 teaspoons chili powder
1 tablespoon tomato paste
2 teaspoons light brown
   sugar
1¼ cups beef broth
1 bay leaf
salt and pepper, to taste
8 fresh bay leaves, to garnish

1 Preheat the oven to 325°.
2 Heat the oil and margarine in a large heatproof Dutch oven. Add the beef and cook over medium heat for about 10 minutes, turning to brown on all sides. Remove and set aside in a warm place.
3 Drain off all but 2 tablespoons fat from the pan. Add the onions, garlic, if using, and carrots and cook very gently for about 10 minutes, stirring occasionally.
4 Stir in chili powder, tomato paste and sugar into the broth, and add the bay leaf. Pour over the onion and carrot mixture in the pan, stir and bring to a boil. Season to taste.
5 Return the beef to the pan and turn it to coat with sauce. Cover and cook in the oven for about 1½ hours, turning occasionally.
6 Transfer the beef to a warmed serving dish. Discard the string and carve the meat into thick slices. Discard the bay leaf and blot all the fat from surface of the liquid (see Watchpoint). Pour into a warmed gravy boat and hand separately with the beef, garnished with bay leaves (see Serving Ideas).

Cook's Notes

TIME
Preparation, including precooking, takes about 20 minutes. Cooking in the oven takes about 1½ hours, finishing about 5 minutes.

WATCHPOINT
As the unstrained cooking liquid is used for the sauce, be sure to blot off all the fat, so that it is not greasy. A crumpled paper towel is ideal for blotting.

SERVING IDEAS
Because the sauce is hot and spicy, it is best to serve this dish with plain vegetables such as boiled cauliflower or potatoes.

●730 calories per portion

Piquant Chuck Roast

SERVES 4
2 lb boneless chuck roast or
  brisket of beef
1 tablespoon beef dripping or
  shortening
2 large onions, thickly sliced
2 large carrots, thickly sliced
1 tablespoon cornstarch
1 tablespoon water

SAUCE
1¼ cups beef broth
3 tablespoons tomato paste
2 tablespoons vinegar
2 tablespoons light brown
  sugar
1 tablespoon country-Dijon
  mustard
1 small onion, finely chopped
1 teaspoon Italian seasoning
salt and pepper, to taste

1 Preheat the oven to 325°.
2 Melt the dripping in a large heat-proof Dutch oven, add the beef and brown on all sides over high heat for 5-10 minutes. Remove the beef, set aside and keep warm.
3 Add the onions and carrots to the pan and cook for 3-4 minutes over medium heat until lightly browned.
4 Meanwhile, mix together all the ingredients for the sauce in a bowl.
5 Return the beef to the pan, pushing the vegetables to the side. Pour the sauce over and bring to a boil. Lower the heat, cover with a tight-fitting lid and transfer to the oven. Cook for about 2 hours or until the beef is tender.
6 Transfer the beef to a warmed serving platter. Remove the vegetables from the sauce with a slotted spoon and place around the meat. Keep hot.
7 Remove any fat from the sauce by blotting it with a paper towel. Mix the cornstarch and water to a paste in a bowl, then gradually stir into the

Cook's Notes

TIME
Preparation takes about 25 minutes, cooking the beef about 2 hours. Finishing the sauce takes 5-10 minutes.

WATCHPOINT
If the Dutch oven lid does not fit tightly, cover the top with aluminum foil before putting on the lid.

●640 calories per portion

sauce in the pan.
8 Place the pan on top of the stove, bring to a boil, stirring, then lower the heat and simmer for 2 minutes until thickened. Taste and adjust seasoning. Pour a little of the sauce over the beef and vegetables, then serve at once with the remaining sauce handed separately.

Pot Roast Brisket

SERVES 4
**2 lb fresh brisket of beef, rolled
and tied**
2 tablespoons margarine or butter
1 onion, quartered
2 large carrots, sliced
2 celery stalks, sliced
2 cups beef broth
½ teaspoon dried thyme
½ teaspoon dried marjoram
1 tablespoon soy sauce
salt and pepper, to taste
4 teaspoons cornstarch
salt, to taste

1 Melt the margarine in a large heat-proof Dutch oven over high heat and brown the brisket on all sides. Transfer the meat to a plate, set aside and keep it warm.

2 Add the onion, carrots and celery to the pan, lower the heat and cook gently for 5 minutes, stirring. Return the meat to the pan and add the broth, thyme, marjoram, soy sauce and pepper to taste.

3 Bring to a boil, then lower the heat, cover and simmer gently for 2½ hours, turning the meat over every 30 minutes (see Watchpoint).

4 When cooked through and tender, remove the meat from the pan and keep warm.

5 Blend the cornstarch to a paste with a little cold water, stir into the pan and bring to a boil. Lower the heat and simmer for 2-3 minutes, stirring constantly, then mash the onions, carrots and celery into the gravy in the pan with a potato masher. Taste and adjust seasoning.

6 Place the meat on a warmed serving platter, cutting a few thin slices from one end, if wished. Pour a little of the gravy over, then serve at once, with the rest handed separately.

Spiced Corned Beef

SERVES 6-8

3-3½ lb corned beef brisket, boned and rolled
pepper, to taste
2 teaspoons ground allspice
2 teaspoons ground nutmeg
½ cup light brown sugar
1 tablespoon whole cloves

1 Put the brisket in a large bowl, pour over fresh cold water to cover and soak for 4 hours, changing the water twice during this time.
2 Preheat the oven to 325°.
3 Drain the brisket and pat dry with paper towels. Season with pepper. Mix together the allspice, nutmeg and sugar and spread all over the brisket, pressing the mixture down with the back of a spoon. Stick cloves all over, then wrap loosely in aluminum foil.
4 Place the brisket in a large Dutch oven, cover and cook in the oven for 3 hours or until the meat is cooked through and juices run clear when the meat is pierced with a skewer.
5 Transfer the brisket, cut side down, to a large plate. Spoon over cooking juices. Cover with foil, place another plate on top and weight down. Leave overnight.
6 Remove the top plate and foil, then transfer the brisket to a carving dish. Remove the string and serve carved into thin slices.

Cook's Notes

TIME
Allow 4 hours soaking time. Preparation then takes 20 minutes, cooking in the oven 3 hours. Allow overnight weighting-down time.

SERVING IDEAS
Serve the sliced brisket with a selection of salads. Try a pasta salad tossed in a mayonnaise dressing with a dash of horseradish sauce or a plain green salad with an oil and vinegar dressing.

●645 calories per portion

Summer Corned Beef Brisket

SERVES 4-6

2½-3¼ lb thick-cut corned beef
  brisket rolled and tied, soaked
  in cold water for 2 hours
2 large carrots, quartered
2 onions, quartered
1 bay leaf
6 whole black peppercorns
1 rounded tablespoon powdered
  unflavored gelatin
⅔ cup hot water
2 tablespoons sherry
watercress and radish waterlilies,
  to garnish

1 Drain and rinse the brisket. Weigh the meat and calculate the cooking time at 25 minutes per 1 lb, plus 25 minutes. Put the brisket in a large saucepan, cover with water and bring to a boil. Skim off scum, then add carrots, onions, bay leaf and peppercorns. Cover the saucepan and simmer the meat gently for the calculated cooking time.

2 When cooked, remove it from the pan and drain. Reserve the cooking liquid. Leave meat until cool enough to handle, then remove the string. Place the corned beef in a 8-9 inch soufflé dish. Place a small plate on top of the beef and weight down. Leave to cool completely, then refrigerate overnight.

3 Sprinkle the gelatin over the hot water in a small heatproof bowl and leave to soak for 5 minutes until spongy, then stand the bowl over a pan of gently simmering water for 1-2 minutes, stirring occasionally, until the gelatin has dissolved. Stir the dissolved gelatin and sherry into the cooking liquid. Remove the plate from the meat and pour the mixture around it. Cover and refrigerate for at least 3 hours, until the gelatin has set completely.

4 Run a round-bladed knife around the edge of the soufflé dish. Invert a round serving dish on top. Hold the dish and plate firmly together and invert them, giving a sharp shake halfway around. Lift away the dish. Serve meat carved into slices, with watercress and radish waterlilies.

Cook's Notes

TIME
Initial preparation time about 5 minutes, cooking about 1½-1¾ hours. Allow overnight chilling time and then a further 3 hours setting time for the gelatin.

SERVING IDEAS
Serve the sliced brisket with salads. Piccalilli (mustard pickle) is an excellent accompaniment.

●740 calories per portion

Walnut-Stuffed Brisket

SERVES 4
2½ lb piece boned brisket of beef
  (see Buying Guide)
2 tablespoons vegetable oil
1 onion, sliced
2 leeks, cut into 1-inch slices
2 carrots, thinly sliced
1 tablespoon tomato paste
beef or chicken broth

FILLING
3 tablespoons margarine or butter
1 onion, finely chopped
⅓ cup finely chopped mushrooms
2 tablespoons soft bread crumbs
½ cup chopped walnuts
salt and pepper, to taste

1 Preheat the oven to 350°.
2 To make the filling, melt the margarine in a small saucepan, add the onion and cook gently for 5 minutes until soft and lightly colored. Add the mushrooms and cook for 5 minutes. Remove from the heat, stir in the bread crumbs and walnuts and season to taste.
3 Place the brisket flat on a board and spread the filling evenly over to within 1 inch of the edges. Press the filling down with the back of a spoon. Roll up from one of the short edges, pressing the meat down gently as you roll, to keep the filling in place. Tie the rolled brisket in several places with fine string.
4 Heat the oil in a heatproof Dutch oven. Add the sliced onion and leeks and cook over moderate heat for 2 minutes, stirring once or twice. Add the carrots, stir and cook for 1 further minute, then add the tomato paste and broth and season. Bring to a boil, stirring, then add the beef.
5 Cover, transfer to the oven and cook for 2½ hours, or until the juices run clear when the brisket is pierced with a sharp knife.
6 Transfer the brisket to a warmed serving platter and remove the string. Remove the vegetables from the pan with a slotted spoon and arrange around the brisket. Strain the cooking liquid.
7 Carve the meat into slices and serve hot, with the strained liquid for a sauce handed separately in a warmed pitcher.

Apricot and Almond Beef

SERVES 4

1½ lb stewing beef, cut into 1-inch cubes (see Buying Guide)
1 tablespoon vegetable oil
4 bacon slices, chopped
2 small onions, sliced
3 tablespoons all-purpose flour
salt and pepper, to taste
1 tablespoon mustard
1 tablespoon black molasses
1 tablespoon tomato paste
1¼ cups beef broth
⅔ cup dried apricots, soaked overnight in ⅔ cup hard cider
2 large carrots, sliced
2 celery stalks, thinly sliced
⅓ cup toasted slivered almonds

1 Preheat the oven to 325°.
2 Heat the oil in a heatproof Dutch oven, add the bacon and cook gently for 2-3 minutes, until the fat runs. Add the onions and cook gently for a further 5 minutes, until soft.

3 Put the flour in a plastic bag and season to taste. Add the beef cubes and shake to coat them thoroughly. Reserve any excess seasoned flour.
4 Add the beef cubes to the pan and cook briskly for 2-3 minutes to brown on all sides. Remove the pan from the heat.
5 In a bowl, blend together the mustard, molasses, tomato paste and broth. Stir into the pan. Drain the cider from the soaked apricots and stir into the pan with the reserved seasoned flour.
6 Chop the apricots into small pieces and add to the pan with the carrots and celery.
7 Return to the heat and bring to a boil, then lower the heat and simmer for 2-3 minutes, stirring.
8 Cover and cook in the oven for about 2 hours, until the meat and vegetables are tender when pierced with a sharp knife.
9 Stir half the toasted almonds into the pan, then taste and adjust the seasoning, if necessary. Serve at once, straight from the Dutch oven, with the remaining almonds sprinkled on top.

Cook's Notes

TIME
Preparation and cook-take about 2½ hours.

BUYING GUIDE
Flank steak would also be a suitable cut.

SERVING IDEAS
Serve with lightly cooked broccoli spears and baked potatoes topped with sour cream and chives.

MICROWAVE
In large casserole, cook onion and bacon on High until tender, stirring. Follow step 3. Add beef to onion. Follow steps 5 and 6. Cover. Cook on High until very hot. Cook on Medium until tender, stirring. Let stand for 10 minutes.

●625 calories per portion

Beef and Bacon Casserole

SERVES 4

1½ lb lean braising steak, trimmed of fat and cut into 1-inch cubes
½ lb bacon slices, cut into 2-inch pieces
1½ lb leeks, roughly chopped
⅔ cup roughly chopped mushrooms
¼ cup beef dripping or shortening
¼ cup all-purpose flour
2½ cups beef broth
2 tablespoons tomato paste
1 tablespoon Worcestershire sauce

1 Preheat the oven to 325°.
2 Roll the bacon pieces around the beef cubes until all the pieces of bacon have been used.

3 Place the leeks and mushrooms in the bottom of a 2-quart heatproof dish or Dutch oven and arrange the beef and bacon rolls in rows on top of the vegetables, together with any remaining beef cubes.
4 Melt the dripping in a saucepan, sprinkle in the flour and stir over low heat for 1-2 minutes, until straw-colored. Gradually stir in the broth, tomato paste and Worcestershire sauce and bring to a boil. Lower the heat and simmer for 2 minutes, stirring frequently until the sauce is thick and very smooth.
5 Pour the sauce over the meat and vegetables in the dish.
6 Cover with aluminum foil or a lid and cook in the oven for 2½-3 hours or until the meat is tender.
7 Blot any fat from the surface of the sauce with paper towels, then serve hot, straight from the dish or Dutch oven (see Serving Ideas).

Cook's Notes

TIME
Preparation takes about 40 minutes, cooking in the oven 2½-3 hours.

SERVING IDEAS
Serve with garden peas or buttered carrots and baked potatoes topped with butter or sour cream.

VARIATIONS
Replace 2 tablespoons of the beef broth with medium-dry sherry. Use a mixture of diced rutabaga, carrot, parsnip and onion instead of leeks and mushrooms.

●655 calories per portion

Beef Goulash

SERVES 4

1 lb chuck steak, cubed
½ lb veal for stewing, cubed
2 tablespoons margarine or butter
2 tablespoons vegetable oil
2 large onions, finely chopped
2 teaspoons sweet paprika
1 x 16 oz can tomatoes, drained
2-3 cups button mushrooms
1¼ cups beef broth
1 tablespoon tomato paste
salt and pepper, to taste
⅔ cup sour cream
1 tablespoon chopped fresh
parsley

1 Preheat the oven to 325°.
2 Heat the margarine and half the oil in a skillet, add the onions and cook without browning over low heat. Drain and remove to a Dutch oven.
3 Add the remaining oil to the pan and cook the meat over high heat, until evenly browned. Sprinkle the paprika over, cook for 1-2 minutes and remove to the Dutch oven.
4 Chop the tomatoes, lay them on top of the meat, and add the whole mushrooms, broth and tomato paste. Season. Cover and cook for about 2-2½ hours, until the meat is tender. Taste and adjust seasoning. Before serving, stir in half the sour cream and pour the rest over the top. Sprinkle with chopped parsley. Serve at once with small boiled new potatoes. Alternatively, serve with mashed potatoes, macaroni and a crisp green vegetable such as broccoli.

Cook's Notes

TIME
Preparation will take 25-30 minutes. Cook the goulash for 2-2½ hours, until the meat is tender when tested with a fork. Goulash is very good when reheated.

MICROWAVE
In large casserole, combine onions and margarine. Cook on High until tender. Add meat, paprika, tomatoes, mushrooms, broth and tomato paste. Season. Stir and cover. Cook on High until very hot. Cook on Medium until meat is tender, stirring occasionally. Let stand for 10 minutes.

•530 calories per portion

Beef Milanese

SERVES 4

1½ lb chuck steak, trimmed and
   cut into ½-inch cubes
3 tablespoons shortening
1 large onion, sliced
1 clove garlic, crushed (optional)
1 green and 1 red pepper, seeded
   and cut into slices
1 x 2 oz can anchovy fillets, drained
   and very finely chopped
1 x 16 oz can tomatoes
½ teaspoon dried basil or
   oregano
pepper, to taste
½ cup pitted Spanish olives
½ cup pitted ripe olives
1 tablespoon cornstarch
1 tablespoon cold water
1 tablespoon tomato paste
salt, to taste

1 Melt the shortening in a heatproof Dutch oven, add the cubed beef and cook over moderate heat for about 5 minutes, until meat is evenly browned on all sides. Remove from the pan with a slotted spoon, set aside on a plate and keep hot.

2 Add the onion, garlic, if using, and peppers to the pan and cook over medium heat until soft.

3 Return the beef to the pan with the anchovies, the tomatoes and their juice, the basil and pepper to taste. Bring to a boil, breaking up the tomatoes with a wooden spoon. Lower the heat, cover and simmer gently for about 1½ hours.

4 Add the olives to the pan, cover and simmer for a further 30 minutes or until beef is tender.

5 Blend the cornstarch with the cold water and stir it into pan, then add the tomato paste and simmer for 2-3 minutes, stirring. Season if necessary. Serve at once, straight from the Dutch oven.

Cook's Notes

TIME
30 minutes preparation; about 2 hours cooking.

SERVING IDEAS
Serve with plain boiled potatoes, pasta or rice.

MICROWAVE
In large casserole combine onion, garlic and peppers. Cover. Cook on High until tender, stirring once. Add beef, anchovies, tomatoes and juice, olives, basil and pepper. Cover. Cook on Medium until beef is tender, stirring occasionally. Blend cornstarch and water. Stir in during last 15 minutes. Let stand 10 minutes.

●515 calories per portion

Beef and Oatmeal Stew

SERVES 4

1 lb lean stewing beef, trimmed of excess fat and cut into 1-inch cubes
¼ cup vegetable oil
2 onions, thinly sliced
3 tablespoons oatmeal, ground
salt and pepper, to taste
2 bouillon cubes
1¼ cups boiling water
1 lb frozen mixed vegetables

1 Preheat the oven to 325°.
2 Heat half the oil in a skillet. Add the onions and cook very gently for 5 minutes until soft and lightly colored (see Microwave). Using a slotted spoon, transfer the onions to a heatproof Dutch oven.
3 Put the oatmeal in a plastic bag and season. Add the beef cubes and shake well to coat the meat thoroughly in the seasoned oatmeal.
4 Heat the remaining oil in the skillet, add the coated beef cubes and cook briskly for a few minutes, stirring until browned on all sides. Using a slotted spoon, transfer the browned beef cubes to the heatproof Dutch oven.
5 Mix together the bouillon cubes and water and pour into the skillet. Bring to a boil, stirring constantly with a wooden spoon to scrape up the sediment from the base of the pan. Pour over the onions and beef.
6 Cover the Dutch oven and cook in the oven for 1½ hours. Add the mixed vegetables and cook for a further 30 minutes or until the beef is tender when pierced with a sharp knife. Serve the stew hot, straight from the pan.

Cook's Notes

TIME
15 minutes preparation; about 2 hours cooking.

MICROWAVE
In large casserole, combine onion and 1 tablespoon oil. Cover. Cook on High until tender. Follow steps 3-5. Cover. Cook on High until very hot. Cook on Medium until beef is tender, stirring occasionally. Add mixed vegetables. Cook 10 minutes longer. Let stand 10 minutes.

SERVING IDEAS
Serve with mashed or baked potatoes.

●400 calories per portion

Beef and Olive Casserole

SERVES 4

1½ lb chuck steak, trimmed of
    excess fat and cut into 1-inch
    cubes
1 tablespoon shortening
2 bacon slices, chopped
1 onion, chopped
2 cloves garlic, crushed (optional)
1 x 16 oz can tomatoes
3 strips orange rind
juice of 1 small orange
¼ teaspoon dried thyme
1 bay leaf
salt and pepper
½ cup pimiento-stuffed Spanish
    olives, halved
finely chopped fresh parsley, to
    garnish (optional)

1 Preheat the oven to 325°.
2 Melt the shortening in a heatproof
Dutch oven, add the bacon and cook
for 3-5 minutes over medium heat,
until crisp. Remove the bacon with a
slotted spoon and set aside to drain
on paper towels (see Microwave).
2 Add the beef cubes to the Dutch
oven and cook briskly for 3-5
minutes, stirring, until browned on
all sides. Remove the beef from the
pan with a slotted spoon and set
aside with the bacon.
4 Add the onion to the pan with the
garlic, if using, and cook gently for 5
minutes, until the onion is soft and
lightly colored. Return the beef and
bacon to the pan and add the canned
tomatoes with their juice, the orange
rind and juice, thyme, bay leaf and
seasoning to taste. Bring to a boil,
stirring, then cover and cook in the
oven for 1 hour.
5 Add the olives to the casserole and
cook for a further 1-1½ hours, until
the meat is very tender when
pierced with a sharp knife. Discard
the orange rind and bay leaf.
Sprinkle with parsley, if liked, and
serve at once. The liquid should be
of a coating consistency. Reduce by
cooking, uncovered, over medium
heat, if necessary.

Cook's Notes

TIME
Preparation takes about
30 minutes, cooking in
the oven about 2-2½ hours.

MICROWAVE
In large casserole, cook
bacon on High until
crisp. Remove bacon with slotted spoon. Set aside. Add
onion and garlic to casserole.
Cook on High until tender.
Add the remaining ingre-
dients. Cover. Cook to boiling.
Cook on Medium until beef is
tender, stirring occasionally.
Let stand 10 minutes.

FREEZE
Transfer to a rigid con-
tainer and cool. Remove
excess fat from surface, freeze
for up to 3 months.

●290 calories per portion

Beef and Pumpkin Stew

SERVES 4-6

1½ lb braising beef steak, cut into
   1½-inch cubes
3 tablespoons margarine or butter
2 onions, sliced
2 cloves garlic, finely chopped
   (optional)
1 large green pepper, seeded and
   finely chopped
6 bacon slices, chopped
1 cup dry red wine
1 bay leaf (see Buying Guide)
salt and pepper, to taste
1 lb pumpkin, peeled and cut
   into 1½-inch cubes

1 Melt the margarine in a large heat-proof Dutch oven. Add the onions, garlic, if using, and green pepper and cook gently for 5 minutes, until softened (see Microwave).

2 Increase the heat slightly, add the beef and bacon and cook, turning, to brown the beef on all sides.

3 Preheat the oven to 325°.

4 Stir in wine, add the bay leaf and season to taste. Bring to a boil, lower heat, cover and simmer for 5 minutes.

5 Add the pumpkin to the pan, bring back to a boil, then transfer the pan to the oven and cook for about 1½ hours or until the beef is tender when pierced with a sharp knife. Taste and adjust seasoning, then serve hot.

Cook's Notes

TIME
Preparation takes about 25 minutes. Precooking takes about 15 minutes, cooking about 1½ hours.

ECONOMY
Instead of wine, use beef broth and add a little tomato paste to it for flavor and color, if liked.

MICROWAVE
In large casserole, cook butter, onion, garlic and green pepper on High until tender, stirring once. Add all the remaining ingredients. Stir. Cover. Cook on High until very hot. Cook on Medium until the beef is very tender, stirring occasionally. Let stand 10 minutes.

BUYING GUIDE
Braising steak is more tender and cooks more quickly than stewing beef.
Dried bay leaves are a handy pantry item, and you can also buy ground bay leaves. ½ teaspoon ground bay leaves is equivalent to a whole leaf.

●485 calories per portion

Beef and Wine Casserole

SERVES 4
1½ lb stewing steak, trimmed
   and cut into 1-inch cubes
¼ cup all-purpose flour
salt and pepper, to taste
2 tablespoons beef dripping or
   shortening
2 onions, sliced
1 clove garlic, crushed (optional)
2 carrots, sliced
⅔ cup red wine
⅔ cup beef broth
¼ cup tomato paste
bouquet garni

TOPPING
4 chunky slices French bread
1-2 tablespoons country-Dijon
   mustard

1 Preheat the oven to 325°.
2 Put the flour in a plastic bag and season. Place the meat in the bag and shake until the meat is well coated with flour. Reserve any excess.
3 Melt the dripping in a Dutch oven, add the onions, garlic, if using, and carrots, and cook over low heat for 5 minutes, until the onions are lightly colored (see Microwave). Remove the vegetables with a slotted spoon and set aside.
4 Add the meat to the cooking juices remaining in the pan and cook over high heat, turning, until browned on all sides. Return the vegetables to the pan and stir in any flour remaining from coating the meat.
5 Gradually blend in the red wine, beef broth and tomato paste. Add the bouquet garni and season.
6 Bring to a boil, stirring. Cover and transfer to the oven. Cook for 2½-3 hours or until tender. Remove from oven and discard bouquet garni.
7 Spread the French bread with mustard and arrange mustard side up, on top of the casserole. Return to the oven, and cook, uncovered, for about 15 minutes more.

Cook's Notes

TIME
20 minutes preparation;
3¼ hours cooking.

FREEZING
Transfer to foil container, cool. Remove excess fat. Freeze for up to 6 months.

MICROWAVE
Follow step 2. In large casserole, combine onions, carrots, garlic and dripping. Cover. Cook on High until carrot is tender, stirring occasionally. Add other casserole ingredients. Cover. Cook on High until very hot. Cook on Medium until beef is tender, stirring occasionally. Let stand for 10 minutes.

●525 calories per portion

Caraway Beef

SERVES 4

1½ lb chuck steak, trimmed of fat
    and gristle and cut across the
    grain into 2 x ½-inch strips
3 tablespoons beef dripping or
    shortening
¼ lb bacon slices, chopped
1 large onion, roughly chopped
2 celery stalks, sliced
2 teaspoons paprika
1 teaspoon caraway seeds
½ teaspoon dried marjoram
1¼ cups beef broth
salt and pepper, to taste
⅔ cup sliced button mushrooms
1 tablespoon cornstarch
1 tablespoon water
little extra paprika, to finish

1 Melt the dripping in a heatproof Dutch oven. Add the beef strips and bacon and cook over medium to high heat for 5 minutes, stirring, until browned all over.

2 Remove the beef and bacon with a slotted spoon and reserve. Add the onion and celery to the pan and cook gently for 5 minutes, stirring once or twice, until the vegetables are soft and lightly colored.

3 Return the beef and bacon to the pan and stir in the paprika, caraway seeds and marjoram. Pour in the broth and season to taste.

4 Bring to a boil, then lower the heat, cover and simmer gently for 1½ hours, stirring occasionally. Stir in the mushrooms, cover and simmer gently for a further 30 minutes, until the meat is very tender when pierced with a sharp knife.

5 In a cup, blend the cornstarch to a smooth paste with the water. Stir into the pan and simmer for 2 minutes, stirring. Taste and adjust seasoning if necessary, then sprinkle lightly with a little extra paprika. Serve the beef at once.

Cook's Notes

TIME
Preparation, including prebrowning the meat and vegetables, takes about 45 minutes. Cooking takes about 2 hours in all.

MICROWAVE
In large casserole, combine onion, celery, bacon and dripping. Cover. Cook on High until tender, stirring once. Add beef, paprika, caraway and marjoram. Cook on Medium until almost tender, stirring once. Add mushrooms. Cover. Cook until the beef is tender. Blend cornstarch and water. Stir into beef. Cook on Medium until bubbly, stirring once.

●460 calories per portion

Chili Beef Rolls

SERVES 4
4 thin slices brisket of beef,
  each weighing ¼ lb
2 tablespoons vegetable oil
1 large green pepper, seeded and
  diced
1 large red pepper, seeded and
  diced
1 onion, finely chopped
2 large slices whole wheat
  bread, crusts removed and
  crumbled
3 tablespoons tomato paste
½ teaspoon mild chili seasoning
  (see Buying Guide)
salt, to taste
1 cup beef broth or water

1 Preheat the oven to 375°.
2 Heat the oil in a skillet, add half
the green and red peppers and the
onion and cook gently for about 5
minutes, until softened. Remove
from the heat (see Microwave).
3 Add the bread to the pan with the
tomato paste, chili seasoning and
salt to taste. Stir well to mix.
4 Lay the brisket slices out flat on a
board or counter top. Spread half the
stuffing mixture evenly over each
slice of meat, then roll up and secure
with wooden cocktail sticks. Place
the beef rolls, seam-side down, in a
single layer in a baking dish or
shallow Dutch oven.
5 Gradually blend the broth into the
remaining stuffing mixture. Taste
and add more seasoning and chili, if
necessary. Pour over the meat.
6 Cover and cook in the oven for 1
hour or until the meat is tender
when pierced with a skewer. Lift the
rolls from the dish with a slotted
spoon and remove the cocktail
sticks. Place the rolls in a warmed
serving dish, pour the sauce over
and garnish with the remaining
diced peppers (if you like, blanch
them by plunging them in boiling
water for 1 minute). Serve.

Cook's Notes

TIME
Preparation 30 minutes,
cooking 1 hour.

MICROWAVE
In small casserole, com-
bine half red and green
peppers and 1 tablespoon oil.
Cover. Cook on High until tender. Follow steps 3-5. Cover
loosely with plastic wrap.
Cook on High until hot. Cook
on Medium until tender. Let
stand 10 minutes.

BUYING GUIDE
Jars of chili seasoning
are available from
supermarkets. Chili seasoning
is a good spice to use if you find
the taste of chili powder too hot
and strong.

●370 calories per portion

Farmer's Beef

SERVES 4
2 lb stewing beef, trimmed of excess fat and cut into 1-inch cubes
2 tablespoons all-purpose flour
salt and pepper, to taste
½ teaspoon Italian seasoning
2 tablespoons margarine or butter
1 tablespoon vegetable oil
1 large onion, sliced
3 cups beef broth
1 bay leaf
1 lb small potatoes
1 cup button mushrooms
1 cup shelled fresh peas, or frozen peas thawed

TO GARNISH
2 tablespoons sour cream
1 teaspoon chopped fresh parsley

1 Preheat the oven to 325°.
2 Put the flour in a plastic bag, season and add the herbs. Add the beef cubes and shake until they are evenly coated. Reserve any excess seasoned flour.
3 Heat the margarine and oil in a heavy-bottomed skillet. Add one-third of the beef cubes and cook over high heat for a few minutes, turning to brown evenly. Using a slotted spoon, transfer the beef to a heat-proof Dutch oven. Cook the remaining beef in 2 batches, and transfer to the Dutch oven (see Microwave).
4 Add the onion to the juices in the skillet and cook gently for 5 minutes, until soft. Pour in the broth, add the bay leaf and bring to a boil. Pour over the meat. Stir well, cover and cook in the oven for 1½ hours.
5 Remove the Dutch oven from the oven, add the potatoes, cover and return the Dutch oven to the oven for a further 45 minutes.
6 Remove from the oven, add the mushrooms and peas, cover again and return to the oven for 15 minutes until tender.
7 Swirl sour cream over the top and sprinkle with parsley. Serve at once straight from the Dutch oven.

Cook's Notes

TIME
Preparation 30 minutes; cooking 2½ hours.

MICROWAVE
In large casserole, combine onion and margarine. Cover. Cook on High until tender, stirring once. Add beef, broth, bay leaf and potatoes. Cover. Cook on Medium until tender, adding peas and mushrooms during last 10 minutes. Let stand 10 minutes.

FREEZING
Transfer to a rigid container at end of step 4, cool, freeze for up to 3 months. To serve, thaw then reheat for 45 minutes in a 350° oven. Omit step 5 and proceed from step 6, adding 1 lb canned or pre-cooked potatoes.

●675 calories per portion

Flemish Beef Casserole

SERVES 4

1½ lb stewing beef or chuck steak,
   trimmed and cut into 1-inch cubes
3 tablespoons vegetable oil
3 medium-sized onions, sliced
¼ lb hickory smoked bacon slices,
   chopped
1 clove garlic, crushed (optional)
2 tablespoons all-purpose flour
1 cup brown ale
½ cup beef broth
1 tablespoon red wine vinegar
1 tablespoon light brown sugar
bouquet garni
salt and pepper, to taste
1 tablespoon finely chopped
   parsley, to garnish

MUSTARD CROUTONS
2 large slices white bread, crusts
   removed, each cut into 4 triangles
2 teaspoons mustard
vegetable oil, for cooking

1 In a heatproof Dutch oven, heat oil over high heat, and cook the meat until evenly brown. Remove with a slotted spoon and keep warm.
2 Lower the heat and cook the onions and bacon, stirring occasionally, for 5-7 minutes until softened and beginning to color. Add the garlic and sauté for 1 minute.
3 Add the flour and stir, scraping the crusty bits off the bottom of the pan. Cook until it begins to brown. Stir in the ale and broth and bring to a boil, stirring. Return the meat to the pan, then add the remaining ingredients, except the parsley. Stir well, reduce the heat, cover and simmer gently over low heat for 1¾-2 hours, until the meat is tender.
4 Spread both sides of the bread triangles or squares with mustard.
5 Heat the oil in a skillet and cook the croutons for a few seconds until they are evenly browned.
6 Drain on paper towels.
7 Serve casserole hot, with parsley and the mustard croutons.

Cook's Notes

 TIME
Preparation 25 minutes, cooking 2 hours.

BUYING GUIDE
Ready-made bouquet garnis are available from most good supermarkets and delicatessens. Remember to remove before serving.

FREEZING
Cool quickly, remove any excess solidified fat and pack in a rigid container or a heavy-duty plastic freezing bag. Seal, label and freeze for up to 3 months. To use, thaw gently over low heat, bring to boiling point and cook for about 20 minutes, until thoroughly heated.

 COOK'S TIPS
This casserole can be cooked in an oven preheated to 350° for the same length of time.
   Like most casseroles, the flavor is improved if it is made one day, cooled, then reheated thoroughly the next day.

MICROWAVE
In large casserole, cook onions and bacon on High until tender. Add garlic. Cook one minute. Stir in flour and ale. Add other ingredients except parsley. Cover. Cook on High until hot. Cook on Medium until tender. Let stand 10 minutes.

●620 calories per portion

180

Frank and Beef Rolls

SERVES 4

8 very thin slices beef bottom
   round, cut from the thin end,
   total weight 1-1¼ lb, trimmed of
   excess fat
pepper, to taste
3-4 teaspoons country-Dijon
   mustard
4 frankfurters, halved lengthwise
2 tablespoons vegetable oil
2 onions, thinly sliced
1 cup halved button mushrooms
1½ cups beef broth
2 tablespoons tomato paste
1 bay leaf
1 teaspoon Italian seasoning
salt, to taste
1 tablespoon cornstarch
3 tablespoons evaporated milk
fresh bay leaves, to garnish

1 Lay the beef slices on a board, cover with a sheet of wax paper and beat out with a rolling pin, until about 5-inches square and ⅛-inch thick. Sprinkle the beef slices with pepper, then spread with mustard.

2 Lay a frankfurter half on each flattened beef slice and roll up. Secure each with a wooden cocktail stick (see Preparation).

3 Heat the oil in a Dutch oven, add the beef rolls and cook over high heat, turning, for 2-3 minutes, until evenly browned. Remove with a slotted spoon and set aside.

4 Add the onions to the pan and cook gently for 3 minutes, stirring. Add the mushrooms and cook for a further 2 minutes. Stir in the broth, tomato paste, bay leaf and herbs and bring to a boil, stirring. Season.

5 Return the rolls to the pan, lower heat, cover tightly and simmer gently for 45 minutes, until the beef is tender, turning rolls once halfway through the cooking time.

6 Lift the beef rolls from the pan with a slotted spoon, transfer to a plate and remove the cocktail sticks. Blend the cornstarch with the evaporated milk to make a smooth paste, stir into the pan and simmer for 2 minutes, stirring constantly. Return the beef rolls to the pan and turn to coat in the sauce. Garnish with bay leaves and serve, straight from the Dutch oven.

Cook's Notes

TIME
Preparation 40 minutes; cooking 50 minutes.

MICROWAVE
Follow steps 1 and 2. Omit step 3. In baking dish, cook onion and 1 tablespoon oil on High until hot. Add mushrooms. Cook until onion is tender. Stir in broth, tomato paste, bay leaf and herbs. Cook to boiling. Place beef rolls in dish. Spoon over sauce. Cover with plastic wrap. Cook on Medium until tender. Remove rolls. Blend cornstarch and milk. Stir into dish. Cook on High until bubbly, stirring.

PREPARATION
To make sure that the beef rolls are secured, "stitch" the rolled beef together with a wooden cocktail stick, along the length of the roll.

●440 calories per portion

181

Parmesan Beef with Eggplant

SERVES 4

1½ lb stewing beef, trimmed
  of fat and cut into 1-inch cubes
2 tablespoons grated Parmesan
  cheese
¼ cup medium-dry sherry
2 tablespoons lemon juice
2 teaspoons chopped fresh tarragon,
  or 1 teaspoon dried tarragon
salt and pepper, to taste
2 tablespoons vegetable oil
3 tablespoons margarine or butter
1 eggplant cut into 1-inch cubes,
  salted, left to stand for 30
  minutes, rinsed and drained
1 green pepper, seeded and
  diced
1 tablespoon all-purpose flour
2 cups beef broth

1 In a large bowl, combine the Parmesan, sherry, lemon juice and the tarragon. Season. Add beef cubes and turn to coat thoroughly. Cover and leave for 4 hours, turning the beef cubes in the marinade from time to time to coat thoroughly.

2 Preheat the oven to 325°.

3 Using a slotted spoon, remove the beef from the bowl, reserving the marinade. Heat the oil and 2 tablespoons of the margarine in a skillet over high heat, add the beef and cook briskly for 2-3 minutes turning to brown on all sides. Transfer to a heatproof Dutch oven.

4 Pat the drained eggplant cubes dry with paper towels. Add to the skillet together with the green pepper and cook gently for 5 minutes, stirring occasionally, until the eggplant is lightly colored. Using a slotted spoon, transfer the vegetables to the Dutch oven.

5 Melt the remaining margarine in the skillet. Sprinkle in the flour and stir over low heat for 1-2 minutes, scraping the base and sides with a wooden spoon. Gradually stir in the broth and the reserved marinade and bring to a boil, then pour over the beef and vegetables.

6 Cover the Dutch oven and cook in the oven for about 2 hours or until the beef is tender when pierced with a sharp knife. Taste and adjust seasoning, if necessary. Serve hot, straight from the Dutch oven.

Cook's Notes

TIME
Allow 4 hours for marinating; salt the eggplant during this time. Preparation then takes 20 minutes, cooking the casserole in the oven takes about 2 hours.

VARIATIONS
Use 2-3 zucchini, sliced, and 1 small red pepper with the Parmesan beef in place of the eggplant.

SERVING IDEAS
This beef and eggplant casserole is ideal for a midweek meal because it can be made the day before and the flavor improves with reheating. Reheat for 1 hour in an oven preheated to 325°. Baked potatoes and a tossed green salad both make suitable accompaniments to Parmesan Beef with Eggplant.

•505 calories per portion

Parsley Dumpling Stew

SERVES 4

1½ lb chuck steak, trimmed and
  cut into 1-inch cubes
¼ cup all-purpose flour
salt and pepper, to taste
2 tablespoons margarine or butter
2 tablespoons vegetable oil
1 onion, roughly chopped
2 large carrots, thinly sliced
2 celery stalks, thinly sliced
2 teaspoons tomato paste
2 teaspoons finely chopped parsley
pinch of cayenne
1¼ cups beef broth
juice of 1 orange

DUMPLINGS

1 cup all-purpose flour
1½ teaspoons baking powder
½ teaspoon salt
2 tablespoons shortening
1 tablespoon finely chopped
  parsley
½ cup milk

1 Put the flour in a plastic bag, season with salt and pepper, then add the meat. Shake the bag vigorously until the meat is well coated.

2 Heat the margarine and 1 tablespoon oil in a large Dutch oven. Add the meat and cook over light heat for about 3 minutes, stirring, until browned on all sides. Cook the meat in batches, if necessary. Remove from the pan and set aside.

3 Heat the remaining oil in the pan, then add the onion, carrots and celery and cook over medium heat for 3 minutes. Return the meat to the pan, then add the tomato paste, parsley, cayenne, broth, orange juice and salt and pepper to taste.

4 Bring to a boil, stirring and scraping up all the sediment from the sides and bottom of the pan with a wooden spoon. Lower the heat, cover and simmer gently 1½-2 hours until the meat is tender.

5 About 10 minutes before the end of cooking time, prepare the dumplings.

Cook's Notes

TIME
45 minutes initial preparation, then 1¾-2¼ hours simmering.

MICROWAVE
Follow step 1. In large casserole, cook butter, onion, celery and carrot, covered, on High until tender. Add other ingredients except dumplings. Cover. Cook on High until boiling. Cook on Medium until tender, stirring occasionally. Follow steps 5 and 6 to covering dish. Cook on High until dumplings are set.

SPECIAL OCCASION
Replace half the beef broth with red wine.

WATCHPOINT
Dumplings are delicious only if they are light and puffy, so don't be heavy-handed when mixing the dough. Stir in the milk quickly and mix as lightly as possible with the knife until the mixture comes together in lumps. Do not cook the dumplings over too high a heat.

●695 calories per portion

Sift the flour, baking powder and salt into a bowl. Cut in the shortening until the mixture resembles coarse bread crumbs. Stir in parsley. Stir in milk to make a sticky dough.

6 Taste and adjust the seasoning of the stew, then drop 2 tablespoons at a time on top of the stew to make 8 dumplings. Cover the pan again and simmer gently for 15 minutes, until the dumplings are puffed up.

7 Serve at once.

Beef with Peanuts

SERVES 4

2 lb chuck steak or stewing steak, trimmed and cut into 1-inch cubes
¼ cup margarine or butter
3 tablespoons crunchy peanut butter
2 large onions, sliced
2 cloves garlic, crushed (optional)
2 tablespoons all-purpose flour
2 cups beef broth
½ cup salted peanuts
1 tablespoon lemon juice
1 tablespoon tomato paste
1 bay leaf
½ teaspoon ground cloves
½ teaspoon ground ginger
pinch of cayenne

1 Melt half the margarine in a heat-proof Dutch oven, stir in the peanut butter, then the onions and garlic, if using. Cook over moderate heat for

Cook's Notes

TIME
This dish takes 15 minutes to prepare and and about 2½ hours to cook.

FREEZING
Transfer to a rigid container, cool quickly, then seal, label and freeze for up to 4 months. To serve, reheat from frozen in a heavy-bottomed saucepan until bubbling, stirring frequently.

MICROWAVE
In large casserole, cook butter, onion and garlic on High until tender. Stir in flour and broth. Add meat and other ingredients. Cover. Cook on High until hot. Cook on Medium until beef is tender, stirring occasionally. Let stand 10 minutes to complete the cooking process.

●680 calories per portion

4-5 minutes, stirring frequently, until the onions are soft. Melt the remaining margarine in the pan, then add the meat and cook for 3-4 minutes or until it is lightly browned on all sides.

2 Sprinkle in the flour and cook for 1-2 minutes, then gradually stir in the broth and bring to a boil. Stir in

⅓ cup peanuts and the remaining ingredients, then lower the heat, cover and cook gently for 2-2½ hours, until tender.

3 Before serving, discard the bay leaf and taste and adjust seasoning. Sprinkle the remaining peanuts over the top of the meat as a garnish, then serve hot from the Dutch oven.

Raisin Beef

SERVES 4

2 lb beef flank, trimmed of excess
    fat, cut in 4 equal pieces (see
    Buying Guide)
¼ cup all-purpose flour
salt and pepper, to taste
1 onion, sliced
⅔ cup dry red wine
1 tablespoon Worcestershire sauce
1 tablespoon steak sauce
2 teaspoons light brown sugar
⅔ cup seedless raisins, soaked for
    1 hour, then drained
watercress sprigs, to garnish

1 Preheat the oven to 300°.
2 Spread the flour out on a large flat plate and season to taste. Turn the beef pieces in the seasoned flour to coat thoroughly.
3 Put the beef pieces into a shallow Dutch oven and arrange the sliced onion on top. Combine the wine, Worcestershire sauce and the mushroom catsup in a bowl and pour over the beef. Cover tightly with aluminum foil, then with the lid. Cook in the oven for about 3 hours, until beef is very tender when pierced with a sharp knife.
4 Using a slotted spoon, transfer the beef to a plate. Strain the liquid into a jug. Leave to cool completely, then cover both and refrigerate overnight. (The fat is easier to remove from the top of the liquid when the dish is completely chilled. Also the flavor of Raisin Beef is much improved if it is heated through, then served the day after cooking.)
5 The next day, preheat the oven to 350°. Remove the fat from the top of the sauce and pour the sauce into a clean Dutch oven. Add the sugar and raisins and bring to a boil, then add the beef. Cover and cook in the oven for 30 minutes, until the beef is heated through and the sauce is bubbling. Garnish with watercress and serve with plain boiled or mashed potatoes and a salad.

Cook's Notes

TIME
Total preparation time about 20 minutes. Allow overnight chilling of the beef and cooking liquid. Total cooking time is about 3½ hours.

MICROWAVE
Follow steps 2 and 3 to pouring mixture over beef. Cover with plastic wrap. Cook on High until hot. Cook on Medium until tender. Let stand 10 minutes. Follow step 4. Remove fat. Place sauce in casserole. Add sugar and raisins. Cover. Cook on Medium-high until hot.

BUYING GUIDE
Beef flank is a fairly inexpensive cut, ideal for casseroles. It is quite fatty but is very suitable for this dish.

●540 calories per portion

Roast Beef Hotpot

SERVES 4

¾ lb cooked roast beef, cut into
    bite-sized pieces (see Cook's Tip)
1½ lb potatoes, peeled
4 tablespoons beef dripping or
    shortening
1 large onion, chopped
2 carrots, sliced
1 turnip, sliced
1 parsnip, sliced
2 large tomatoes, peeled and
    chopped
½ cup chopped mushrooms
3 tablespoons all-purpose flour
2 cups beef broth (see Cook's Tip)
salt and pepper, to taste

1 Preheat the oven to 375°.
2 Parboil the potatoes for 10
minutes, drain and when they are
very cool, slice them and reserve.
3 Melt 3 tablespoons of the beef
dripping in a large skillet, add the
onion and cook gently until soft and
lightly colored.
4 Stir in the remaining vegetables,
except the potatoes and cook gently
until lightly colored.
5 Add the meat, sprinkle over the
flour, then increase the heat and
cook for a further 3 minutes, stirring
constantly until the meat is lightly
browned on all sides.
6 Stir in the broth, bring to a boil and
stir until the mixture thickens. Season
to taste.
7 Transfer the meat and vegetables
to a 2-quart Dutch oven or heatproof
dish. Arrange the sliced potatoes in
layers on the top and sprinkle with
salt and peper.
8 Dot with the remaining dripping
and cook in the oven for 1 hour, until
the potatoes are golden brown.
Serve the dish hot, straight from
the Dutch oven.

Cook's Notes

TIME
Preparation and cooking
time is 1½ hours.

COOK'S TIP
This dish is perfect for
using up any cold left-
over beef. Pork or lamb can be
used in the same way. Leftover
gravy can be used too, to give
extra flavor to the broth of the
Roast Beef Hotpot.

SERVING IDEAS
Serve with a simple
green vegetable such
as Savoy cabbage or Brussels
sprouts. Horseradish sauce is
also a good accompaniment to
Roast Beef Hotpot.

●510 calories per portion

Serbian Beef

SERVES 4-5

2 lb stewing beef, trimmed and
   cut into bite-sized pieces
2 tablespoons beef dripping or
   shortening
2 large onions, sliced
1 tablespoon paprika
1 celery stalk, chopped
2 cloves garlic, crushed (optional)
1 bay leaf
1 tablespoon chopped parsley
salt and pepper, to taste
⅔ cup red wine vinegar
4 potatoes, thinly sliced
vegetable oil, for brushing

1 Preheat the oven to 300° and
lightly brush a large heatproof dish
with oil.
2 Melt half the dripping in a heavy-
bottomed heatproof Dutch oven
over high heat and cook the meat in
batches, if necessary, until crisp and
golden on all sides. Use a slotted
spoon to transfer the meat to a plate,
set aside and keep warm.
3 Add the remaining dripping to the
pan and cook the onions gently for
about 5 minutes, until soft.
4 Return the meat and any juices to
the pan. Add the paprika and stir
over low heat for 2 minutes.
5 Add the celery, garlic, if using,
bay leaf, parsley, salt and pepper to
taste and the wine vinegar. Bring to
a boil, remove from the heat and
allow to cool for a few minutes.
6 Put half the potatoes in a layer on
the bottom of the prepared dish,
cover with the meat mixture, and
then add the remaining potatoes in a
neat layer on top. Cover tightly with
a lid or aluminum foil and cook in
the oven for about 2½ hours, until
the meat is tender.
7 Brush the potatoes with vegetable
oil and place the casserole under a
preheated high broiler for 5 minutes,
until the potatoes are browned.
Serve hot straight from the dish.

Cook's Notes

TIME
Preparation takes 30
minutes; cooking takes
about 2½ hours.

VARIATIONS
Use other vegetables
such as thinly sliced
leeks and carrots.

COOK'S TIP
Wine vinegar helps
tenderize the beef and
adds a pleasant piquancy to the
Serbian Beef.

DID YOU KNOW
As its name suggests,
this dish is traditional
in eastern Europe. It provides a
hearty meal, particularly wel-
come in cold weather.

●645 calories per portion

Spanish Beef Casserole

SERVES 4

1 lb stewing steak, cut into 1½-inch cubes
2 tablespoons olive or vegetable oil
1 onion, chopped
1 clove garlic, crushed (optional)
1 x 16oz can chopped tomatoes
1 red pepper, seeded and chopped
2 tablespoons medium-dry sherry
8 stuffed Spanish olives, halved
½ teaspoon dried thyme
salt and pepper, to taste

TOPPING

1 tablespoon butter
1 small onion, finely chopped
1 cup long grain rice
1¼ cups boiling water
1 tablespoon grated Parmesan cheese

1 Preheat the oven to 350°.

2 Put olive oil in large heatproof Dutch oven, add the onion, garlic and meat and cook for 5 minutes.

3 Add the tomatoes, half the red pepper, the sherry, Spanish olives and thyme, and season to taste. Bring to a boil, cover, then transfer to the oven and cook for 1¼ hours.

4 To make topping, melt the butter in a large saucepan, add onion and cook gently for 5 minutes, until soft.

5 Add the rice and stir until coated with butter. Add the remaining red pepper and season with salt, if desired. Add the boiling water, then cover and simmer for about 10-15 minutes, until the rice is tender and all the liquid has evaporated. Remove from heat and stir in the grated Parmesan cheese.

6 Spread the topping evenly over the meat in the Dutch oven. Return to the oven and cook, uncovered, for a further 20 minutes. Serve at once (see Serving Ideas).

Cook's Notes

TIME
Preparing and cooking take about 2 hours.

SERVING IDEAS
Serve the Spanish Beef Casserole with buttered cabbage for a complete meal.

MICROWAVE
In large casserole, combine oil, onion and garlic. Cover. Cook on High until onion is tender, stirring once. Add beef, tomatoes, half pepper, sherry, olives, thyme, seasoning. Cover. Cook on High until boiling. Cook on Medium until beef is tender, stirring. Let stand 10 minutes.

●505 calories per portion

Spiced Peking Beef

SERVES 4

1 lb beef chuck steak, trimmed of excess fat and cut into 2 x ½-inch slices
1 tablespoon country-Dijon mustard
3 tablespoons all-purpose flour
salt and pepper, to taste
2 tablespoons vegetable oil
1 cup water
2 tablespoons soy sauce
1½ tablespoons light brown sugar
2 teaspoons Worcestershire sauce
1½ tablespoons tomato paste
1 onion, chopped
1 celery stalk, finely chopped

1 Preheat the oven to 300°.

2 Put the mustard in a bowl, add the beef slices and stir until they are well coated.

3 Spread the flour out on a flat plate and season. Dip each piece of beef in the seasoned flour until thoroughly and evenly coated.

4 Heat the oil in a large skillet, add the beef slices and cook over brisk heat, stirring, for about 2 minutes, until browned on all sides. Remove from the pan with a slotted spoon and place in a shallow heatproof Dutch oven or dish.

5 Stir all the remaining ingredients into the fat in the skillet, bring to a boil, then pour over the beef slices in the Dutch oven.

6 Stir once, cover the dish and cook in the oven for 1 hour. Remove from the oven and stir again. Return to the oven, uncovered, and cook for a

further 1½ hours, stirring every 30 minutes. Serve hot.

Avocado Beef

SERVES 4
1 lb lean ground beef
1-2 tablespoons vegetable oil
1 small onion, finely chopped
1-2 teaspoons chili powder
2 tablespoons quick-cooking
  rolled oats
1¼ cups beef broth
1 tablespoon tomato paste
pinch of freshly ground nutmeg
salt and pepper, to taste
1 x 14 oz can whole kernel corn
  with sweet peppers, drained
1 large or 2 medium avocados
1 tablespoon lemon juice
¼ lb Cheddar cheese, cut into
  1-inch cubes

1 Heat 1 tablespoon oil in a heavy-bottomed saucepan. Add the beef and cook over medium heat for 3 minutes, stirring constantly, until all the beef has browned, breaking up any lumps with a wooden spoon. Remove the beef with a slotted spoon. Add the onion to the pan and cook for 5 minutes, until soft and lightly colored, adding a further tablespoon oil if necessary.

2 Return the beef to the pan, stir in chili powder to taste, then the oats, broth, tomato paste, nutmeg, salt to taste and a sprinkling of pepper.

3 Bring to a boil, stirring, then lower the heat, cover and simmer gently for 40-45 minutes or until the oats are soft and the meat cooked.

4 Stir the drained corn and peppers into the beef mixture and continue to cook, uncovered, for 5 minutes until most of the excess liquid has evaporated. Taste and adjust seasoning, adding more chili if a slightly hotter flavor is desired.

5 Just before serving, cut the avocado in half lengthwise and discard the seed. Cut into quarters lengthwise and peel away the skin, then cut the flesh into neat thin slices. Brush with the lemon juice to prevent discoloration.

6 Stir the cheese into the beef until just beginning to melt, then spoon the mixture into a warmed serving dish and arrange the avocado slices around the edge. Serve at once.

Cook's Notes

 TIME
Preparation 30 minutes, cooking 45 minutes.

VARIATION
If you do not have any chili powder (available in jars from most supermarkets), use the same quantity of mild curry powder; this will season the beef, but will not give a strong curry flavor.

MICROWAVE
In medium casserole, combine beef and onion. Cook on High until beef is set and onion is tender, stirring occasionally. Drain. Follow step 2. Cover. Cook on High until boiling. Cook on Medium until oats are soft, stirring once. Stir in corn and peppers. Cook, uncovered, on High until excess liquid evaporates.

●555 calories per portion

Beef and Bean Turnovers

MAKES 6
PASTRY
1 package (10 oz) pie crust mix
water, to mix
1 small egg, beaten, to glaze

FILLING
¾ lb lean ground beef
2 tablespoons Worcestershire sauce
1 tablespoon tomato sauce
1 medium onion, finely chopped
2 tablespoons chopped parsley
1 tablespoon chopped fresh thyme,
   or 1 teaspoon dried thyme
salt and pepper, to taste
1 x 8 oz can baked beans in
   tomato sauce

1 Prepare the dough according to the package directions. Wrap in plastic wrap and chill for 30 minutes.
2 Preheat the oven to 350°.
3 To make the filling, put the beef into a bowl and stir in the Worcestershire sauce, tomato sauce, onion, herbs and salt and pepper. Mix well. Fold in the beans carefully.
4 Divide the dough into 6 pieces and roll on a floured board into 7-inch circles. Use a side plate of the correct diameter to trim the dough. Lay a portion of the filling to one side of each circle. Brush the edges of the dough with water, fold the dough over the filling, then press the edges together to seal them.
5 Place the turnovers on floured cookie sheets and brush them with the beaten egg. Prick each turnover 4 times with a fork. Bake in the oven for 45 minutes. Serve hot or cold.

Cook's Notes

TIME
Preparation 35 minutes, cooking 45 minutes. Allow 30 minutes to chill the dough thoroughly.

WATCHPOINT
Prick the turnovers so the steam can escape and turnovers will not burst.

SERVING IDEAS
Serve the turnovers hot with catsup or steak sauce. Cold turnovers make substantial and delicious additions to a lunchbox.

● 600 calories per portion

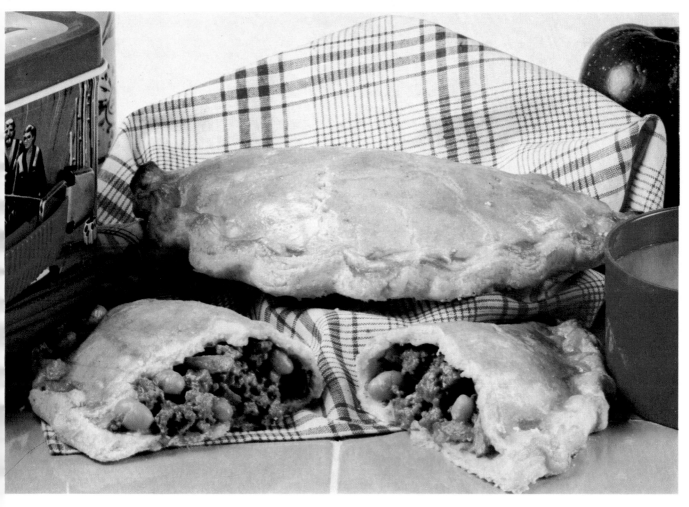

Beef and Celery Bake

SERVES 4
1½ lb lean ground beef
1 tablespoon margarine or butter
1 tablespoon vegetable oil
4 celery stalks, chopped
2 cups sliced mushrooms
1 tablespoon catsup
1 x 10¾ oz can cream of celery soup
salt and pepper, to taste
margarine, for greasing

BATTER
1 cup all-purpose flour
2 eggs
⅔ cup milk
3 tablespoons water

1 Preheat the oven to 400°. Grease a baking dish (see Microwave).
2 Heat the margarine and oil in a large saucepan, add the celery and cook gently until it is softened.
3 Add the ground beef to the pan and cook until the meat is evenly browned, stirring with a wooden spoon to remove any lumps. Stir in the mushrooms and cook for a further 1-2 minutes.
4 Stir in the catsup and the celery soup. Stir well until the mixture is simmering. Continue to cook over a low heat, stirring from time to time for 5-10 minutes. Season to taste and pour into the prepared baking dish. Level the surface.
5 To make the batter, sift the flour with a pinch of salt into a large bowl and make a well in the center. Beat the eggs with the milk and water and gradually add to the bowl working the flour into the center. Beat to make a smooth batter.
6 Carefully spoon the batter on top of the beef, then cook for 25-30 minutes, until the batter is well risen and brown on top. Serve at once.

Cook's Notes

TIME
Preparation and cooking take 1 hour.

SERVING IDEAS
Potatoes do not need to be served with this dish – the batter makes it filling.

MICROWAVE
Follow step 1. In medium casserole, combine celery and beef. Cook on High until meat is set and celery is tender, stirring occasionally. Stir in mushrooms, catsup and soup. Cook on High until bubbly, stirring once. Turn into greased baking dish.

●595 calories per portion

Beef with Crispy Topping

SERVES 4
1 lb lean ground beef
1 tablespoon vegetable oil
3 onions, sliced
¼ cup all-purpose flour
2 teaspoons dry mustard powder
1 x 16 oz can tomatoes
⅔ cup beef broth
pepper, to taste
¼ cup seedless raisins

TOPPING
2 small packages plain potato chips
½ cup shredded Cheddar

1 Heat the oil in a large skillet with a lid, add the onions and cook gently for 10 minutes, stirring occasionally, until browned. Add the ground beef and cook, constantly stirring with a wooden spoon to remove any lumps, for 5-10 minutes, until the beef has lost all it pinkness. Remove from the heat.

2 In a bowl, mix the flour and dry mustard to a smooth paste with a little of the tomato juice from the can. Stir in the tomatoes with the remaining juice from the can and the beef broth.

3 Add the tomato mixture to the pan and return to the heat. Bring to a boil, stirring constantly. Continue to cook for 1-2 minutes, stirring until the mixture thickens. Lower the heat and season to taste with pepper; stir in the raisins, cover and simmer for a further 20 minutes.

4 Preheat the broiler to high.

5 Spoon the ground mixture into a large shallow baking dish. Sprinkle the potato chips evenly over the surface, then sprinkle the shredded cheese on top.

6 Broil for 2-3 minutes, until the cheese is melted and bubbling and the topping is golden brown. Serve at once, straight from the dish.

Cook's Notes

TIME
Preparing and cooking the dish takes 1 hour.

MICROWAVE
In casserole, combine beef and onion. Cook on High until beef is set and onion tender, stirring often. Follow step 2. Add tomato mixture and raisins. Cook on High until thickened and raisins are soft, stirring.

FOR CHILDREN
This is a very filling meal – and one that is ideal for children, perhaps with the dry mustard omitted.

WATCHPOINT
Do not season with any salt because the potato chips should add sufficient salt to make the dish tasty.

●490 calories per portion

Beef and Leek Patties

SERVES 4
1 lb lean ground beef
1 lb small leeks (see Cook's Tip)
salt, to taste
1 cup day-old white bread crumbs
finely grated rind of 1 lemon
½ teaspoon ground bay leaves
pepper, to taste
2 small eggs, slightly beaten
flour, for coating
2 tablespoons butter
1 tablespoon vegetable oil
4 small thin leeks, to garnish

SAUCE
juice of 2 lemons
⅔ cup hard cider or applejack
⅔ cup water

1 Add the leeks to boiling salted water and cook until just tender.
2 Meanwhile, put the ground beef in a large bowl and mash well with a wooden spoon to make a smooth, sticky paste. Stir in the bread crumbs, rind and ground bay leaves.
3 Drain the leeks thoroughly, then chop finely. Drain again on paper towels and add to the meat. Season and stir in the beaten eggs. Beat well until the mixture is smooth. Cover the bowl with plastic wrap and refrigerate for at least 30 minutes to firm up the patties.
4 Meanwhile, prepare the leek frills. Plunge the prepared leeks into a bowl of ice water and leave for about 30 minutes, until they curl.
5 With floured hands, shape 1 tablespoon of beef into a patty about ½-inch thick. Make a further 7 patties.
6 Spread the flour out on a plate. Dip the patties in the flour to coat.
7 Heat butter and oil in a skillet with a lid, add patties. Cook over medium heat for 4-5 minutes on each side.
8 Add the juice, cider and water to the skillet and season to taste. Bring sauce to a boil. Lower heat, cover and simmer for 15 minutes.
9 Meanwhile, remove the leek frills from the water and pat dry.
10 Remove the patties from skillet and arrange on a warmed dish. Pour sauce over and garnish with leek frills. Serve at once.

Cook's Notes

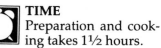

TIME
Preparation and cooking takes 1½ hours.

COOK'S TIP
Use only the white center parts of the leeks for this dish. Reserve the tough outer leaves to make soup.

PREPARATION
To make leek frills:

Trim roots and tops from leeks and remove outer leaves. From top of leek make 8 lengthwise slits about 2½ inches long.

●380 calories per portion

Beef Moussaka

SERVES 4

1 lb lean ground beef
1 tablespoon vegetable oil
1 large onion, chopped
1 teaspoon Italian seasoning
½ cup all-purpose flour
⅓ cup chicken broth
1 x 14 oz can evaporated milk
⅔ cup milk
2 tablespoons margarine or butter
salt and pepper, to taste
2 large eggs, separated
1 lb potatoes, boiled and thinly
  sliced
½ lb zucchini, boiled and thinly
  sliced
parsley sprigs, to garnish

1 Preheat the oven to 350°.
2 Heat the oil in a saucepan, add the onion, ground beef and herbs and stir over medium heat until browned. Stir in 2 teaspoons of the flour and cook for 1 minute. Gradually add the broth, stirring constantly. Cook gently for 15 minutes,

stirring often (see Microwave).
3 Meanwhile, to make the topping, pour the evaporated milk into a measuring cup and add enough milk to make up to 2½ cups. Melt the margarine in a small saucepan, sprinkle in the remaining flour and stir over low heat for 1-2 minutes, until straw-colored. Remove from the heat and gradually stir in the milk from the measuring cup. Return to the heat and simmer, stirring until thick and smooth. Remove from heat and season with salt and pepper. Cover tightly with plastic wrap and leave to cool.
4 Stir the egg yolks into the sauce. In a separate bowl, beat the egg whites until stiff then fold into the sauce.
5 To assemble the moussaka, spread half the ground beef mixture over the base of a baking dish. Cover with half the potato slices, then the zucchini, the remaining potato slices and finally remaining beef mixture. Pour the sauce over the top and bake in the oven for 40-45 minutes, until risen and golden brown. Remove from the oven and leave to stand for 10-15 minutes (see Cook's Tip). Garnish with parsley; serve straight from the dish while hot.

Cook's Notes

TIME
Preparation and cooking take 1½ hours. Allow 15 minutes before serving.

COOK'S TIP
If the moussaka is left to stand for at least 15 minutes, the "egg custard" settles and the moussaka cuts much more easily. Otherwise the topping is too sloppy.

WATCHPOINT
Add yolks to cooled sauce or it will curdle.

MICROWAVE
Follow step 1. In medium casserole, combine beef, onion and herbs. Cook on High until meat is set and onion tender, stirring often. Stir in flour and broth. Cook on Medium-high until bubbly, stirring several times.

●720 calories per portion

Beef and Mushroom Charlotte

SERVES 4-6
1½ lb lean ground beef
1 tablespoon vegetable oil
1 large onion, chopped
1 cup soft white bread crumbs
1¼ cups beef broth
2 tablespoons tomato paste
1 tablespoon Worcestershire sauce
1 tablespoon mustard
salt and pepper, to taste
2 tablespoons all-purpose flour
2 tablespoons water
8 slices whole wheat bread, crusts
    removed
3 tablespoons margarine or butter,
    softened
2¼ cups chopped mushrooms
¼ cup shredded Cheddar cheese
margarine, for greasing

1 Heat the oil in a large heavy-bottomed saucepan, add the ground beef and onion and cook over medium to high heat for about 3-4 minutes, stirring until the beef has lost its pinkness.
2 Stir in the bread crumbs, broth, tomato paste, Worcestershire sauce, mustard and salt and pepper.
3 Bring to a boil, stirring, then lower the heat, cover the pan and simmer gently until the meat is tender.
4 Blend the flour with the water, stir into the pan and stir over low heat until thickened.
5 Preheat the oven to 375°.
6 Butter the slices of bread and cut each slice into 3 fingers. Lightly grease a 1½-quart baking dish or soufflé dish. Use 12 of the bread fingers, buttered side down, to line the bottom and sides of the dish.
7 Scatter half the mushrooms over the bottom of the lined dish. Pour in the beef mixture, then scatter the remaining mushrooms over the surface. Arrange the remaining bread fingers, buttered side up, over the top, sprinkle with the cheese.
8 Bake for 30 minutes, until crisp and golden. Serve at once.

Cook's Notes

TIME
Preparation and cooking the ground beef on top of the stove take about about 50 minutes. Assembling the Charlotte then takes 10 minutes and cooking 30 minutes.

BUYING GUIDE
Buy best-quality lean ground beef to prevent the dish from being greasy.

MICROWAVE
In medium casserole, cook beef and onion on High until beef is set and onion is tender, stirring occasionally. Follow step 2. Cook to boiling. Blend flour and water. Stir into meat. Cover. Cook on Medium until meat is tender, stirring several times.

●675 calories per portion

Beef and Potato Roll

SERVES 4
¾ lb lean ground beef
2⅔ cups dry mashed potato flakes
2⅔ cups water
salt, to taste
6 tablespoons margarine
1 egg, beaten
pepper, to taste
1 small onion, finely chopped
1 green pepper, seeded and
    finely chopped
1 tablespoon tomato catsup
1 teaspoon Italian seasoning
margarine, for greasing
flour, for dusting
paprika (optional)

1 Preheat the oven to 350°. Lightly heat a cookie sheet.
2 Place the potato flakes into a mixing bowl. In a saucepan, bring the water, salt and 5 tablespoons margarine to a boil, then stir into the potato flakes. Let sit for 30 seconds to 1 minute, then stir in the egg. Season to taste and refrigerate for at least 30 minutes.
3 Meanwhile combine the beef, onion, green pepper, tomato catsup and herbs in a bowl and season with salt and pepper.
4 Sift a little flour over a large sheet of wax paper and spoon the potato on top. With a spatula, pat out the potato to a 12 x 9-inch oblong. Sprinkle the potatoes with a little flour if sticky.
5 Spread the beef mixture evenly over the potato to within 1-inch of the edges then, starting from a short end, roll up mixture like a jelly roll. Seal potato ends.
6 Using the paper, carefully transfer the roll to the prepared cookie sheet. Remove the paper. Flake remaining margarine over roll and bake in the oven for 1¼ hours, until the potato is firm and golden.
7 Sprinkle the top with paprika, if liked, then serve at once, garnished with tomato wedges and parsley.

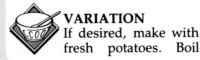

Cook's Notes

TIME
Preparation and cooking take 1¾ hours. Allow 30 minutes chilling.

VARIATION
If desired, make with fresh potatoes. Boil 1½ lb peeled potatoes until tender, then mash with ½ cup margarine. Beat in the egg and seasoning, wrap in plastic wrap and refrigerate for about 30-60 minutes.

●450 calories per portion

Beef and Spinach Savory

SERVES 4
1 lb lean ground beef
1 tablespoon butter
1 tablespoon vegetable oil
1 large onion, chopped
1 x 8 oz can chopped tomatoes
1 tablespoon tomato paste
1 tablespoon catsup
salt and pepper, to taste
½ lb vermicelli (see Variation)
1¼ lb frozen chopped spinach
1 large egg
1 tablespoon grated Parmesan
   cheese
½ teaspoon ground nutmeg
⅔ cup sour cream
2 cups sliced mushrooms
2 large tomatoes, sliced
⅔ cup shredded Cheddar cheese
margarine, for greasing

1 Heat the butter and oil in a large saucepan, add the onion and cook gently for 5 minutes, until soft and lightly colored. Add the ground beef, turn the heat to high and cook for a further 5 minutes or until the meat has lost all its pinkness, stirring with a wooden spoon.

2 Add the tomatoes with their juice, tomato paste and catsup. Stir well, bring to a boil and season. Lower the heat, cover and simmer for about 30 minutes.

3 Meanwhile, bring a large sauce-pan of salted water to a boil, add the vermicelli and cook for about 5 minutes, until just tender. Cook the frozen spinach according to package.

4 Preheat the oven to 350°. Grease a shallow baking dish.

5 Drain the vermicelli and cut up roughly (see Preparation). Beat the egg and Parmesan cheese together in a bowl, and season with pepper and nutmeg. Add the chopped vermicelli and fork it through well. Spoon over base of dish.

6 Drain the spinach and put it into a bowl. Stir in the sour cream.

7 Spoon the beef and tomato mixture over the vermicelli. Arrange the sliced mushrooms on top and evenly spoon over the spinach mixture.

8 Top with the tomato slices and sprinkle with the shredded cheese. Cook in the oven for 20-30 minutes, until the cheese topping is golden.

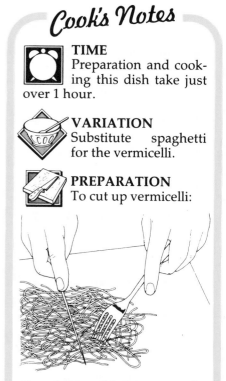

Cook's Notes

TIME
Preparation and cooking this dish take just over 1 hour.

VARIATION
Substitute spaghetti for the vermicelli.

PREPARATION
To cut up vermicelli:

Use a knife and fork to cut up the vermicelli roughly on a wooden chopping board.

●635 calories per portion

Bitkis

SERVES 4
¾ lb lean ground beef
1 large onion, finely chopped
3 cups soft bread crumbs
3 tablespoons freshly chopped
   parsley
salt and pepper, to taste
1 x 8oz can tomatoes
⅔ cup sour cream
vegetable oil
chopped fresh parsley, to garnish

1 In a bowl, mix together the beef, onion, half the bread crumbs, the freshly chopped parsley and the salt and pepper to taste.
2 Divide the mixture into 12 and form each piece into a flat cake with your hands. Toss each cake in the remaining bread crumbs to coat thoroughly and evenly.
3 Heat a little oil in a large skillet and panfry the bitkis for 5 minutes, turning once, until they are golden brown and crispy. Keep them warm over a very low heat while preparing the sauce.
4 Put the tomatoes and sour cream in the goblet of a blender and work until smooth or sieve the tomatoes through a strainer and beat in the cream. Season well, then pour the mixture into a saucepan and heat very gently until barely bubbling.
5 Arrange the bitkis on a serving dish and pour the sauce over them. Garnish with parsley and serve at once with boiled rice and salad.

Cook's Notes

TIME
Preparing and cooking take a total of no more than 25 minutes.

WATCHPOINTS
Take care when panfrying the bitkis, as they could easily break up.
   Do not allow the sauce to boil, as this will make the sour cream curdle.

COOK'S TIP
This tomato sauce is one of the simplest sauces to make, as it does not require thickening and takes only a few seconds. Use it with other favorite vegetable or meat recipes, varying amount of seasoning to taste.

●140 calories per portion

199

Border Shepherd's Pie

SERVES 4

1¾ lb lean ground beef
2 tablespoons vegetable oil
2 large onions, finely chopped
1 cup finely chopped mushrooms
4 tomatoes, finely chopped
1 tablespoon tomato paste
¼ cup all-purpose flour
¼ cup water
1 teaspoon ground cumin
½ teaspoon dried savory
½ teaspoon dried thyme
salt and pepper, to taste
1½ lb potatoes, peeled and cut into chunks
1 lb rutabaga, sliced
1 tablespoon butter

1 Heat the oil in a large skillet, add the onions and cook gently for 10 minutes, until browned. Add meat, turn the heat to high and cook until the meat is evenly browned, stirring with a wooden spoon to remove any lumps. Stir in the mushrooms, tomatoes and tomato paste and cook the mixture for a further 2-3 minutes (see Microwave).

2 Sprinkle the flour into the skillet, then stir in the water, cumin and herbs. Season to taste. Bring to a boil, then lower heat and simmer the meat, uncovered, for about 30 minutes (see Microwave).

3 Meanwhile, preheat the oven to 400°. Bring a pan of salted water to a boil, add the potatoes and rutabaga and cook for 10 minutes, until tender. Drain well and mash thoroughly to remove any lumps. Add the butter and season to taste. Set aside.

4 Spoon the cooked meat mixture into the base of a 1¼-quart baking dish. Spread the mashed potato and rutabaga mixture over the top, then draw a fork over the mixture to make a decorative pattern. Bake in the oven for 20-30 minutes, until pie is well browned and bubbling.

Cook's Notes

TIME
Preparing and cooking take 1½ hours.

MICROWAVE
In medium casserole, cook beef and onion on High until beef is set and onion is tender, stirring often. Add ingredients as step 1. Cook on High until hot. Blend in flour, water, cumin, salt. Cook on High until bubbly, stirring.

VARIATION
In the summer, use tomato paste to color and flavor the potatoes instead of rutabaga. Increase the potato to 2 lb and mix with 3 tablespoons tomato paste.

DID YOU KNOW
Originally shepherd's pie was made with cooked ground lamb left over from the Sunday lunch.
All over Scotland, rutabaga (known as "neeps") are particularly popular and are often served with mashed potatoes.

SERVING IDEAS

Serve with a green vegetable such as peas, winter cabbage or broccoli.

●655 calories per portion

Chili Beef

SERVES 4

1 lb lean ground beef
2 tablespoons vegetable oil
2 onions, finely chopped
1 red pepper, seeded and cut into
  2 × ½-inch strips
1 clove garlic, crushed (optional)
2 tablespoons all-purpose flour
1 teaspoon chili powder, or to
  taste
1 teaspoon ground cumin
1 teaspoon dried oregano
1 tablespoon tomato paste
1 × 8 oz can tomatoes
1¼ cups beef broth
salt, to taste
1 × 17 oz can cannellini beans,
  drained and rinsed (see Economy)

1 Heat the oil in a large heavy-bottomed skillet, add the onions, red pepper and garlic, if using, and cook gently for 5 minutes, until the onion and pepper are soft.
2 Add the beef, turn the heat to high

and cook until the meat is evenly browned, stirring with a wooden spoon to remove lumps.
3 Remove from the heat and stir in the flour, chili powder, cumin and oregano. Add the tomato paste, the tomatoes with their juice and the beef broth.
4 Return to the heat and bring to a

boil, stirring. Season with salt, if desired, but not with pepper (chili powder flavors the dish).
5 Cover the pan and simmer for approximately 40 minutes.
6 Stir in the cannellini beans and simmer for a further 5 minutes to heat through. Turn into a warmed serving dish and serve at once.

Cook's Notes

TIME
Chili takes about 1 hour 20 minutes to prepare and cook.

MICROWAVE
In medium casserole, cook beef, pepper, onion and garlic on High until meat is set and onion is tender, stirring often. Stir in flour, chili powder, cumin, oregano, tomato paste, tomatoes and juice, salt and broth. Cook on High until bubbly. Cook on Medium until flavors blend. Stir in beans. Heat on Medium.

VARIATIONS
If you prefer, use half a green and half a red pepper to add color to the dish.

ECONOMY
Use dried red kidney beans rather than the cannellini beans. Soak the beans in cold water overnight. The next day, cover with fresh water and bring to a boil. Boil for 10 minutes, then simmer for 1 hour until tender. Add the beans to the chili.

●455 calories per portion

Curried Meatballs

SERVES 4
1 lb lean ground beef
2 tablespoons tomato catsup
2 teaspoons Worcestershire sauce
2 teaspoons mustard
2 teaspoons mild curry powder
1 teaspoon salt, or to taste
1 cup soft white bread crumbs
1 tablespoon vegetable oil
1 small onion, finely chopped
1 egg, beaten
vegetable oil, for cooking

1 Put the ground beef, the tomato catsup, the Worcestershire sauce, mustard, curry powder, salt and bread crumbs in a bowl and stir well to mix (see Microwave).

2 Heat the oil in a saucepan, add the onion and cook for 5 minutes, until soft and lightly colored. Remove from the heat and stir into the ground beef mixture until mixed (see Microwave).

3 Add beaten egg to bind the mixture together. Stir thoroughly.

4 Take teaspoons of the prepared mixture and roll into about 30 small balls between floured hands.

5 Preheat the oven to 225°.

6 Heat a little oil in a large skillet; add half the meatballs and cook gently for 8-10 minutes, turning occasionally, until golden brown and cooked through. Drain well on paper towels and keep hot in the oven while cooking the remaining meatballs in the same way.

7 Pile the meatballs onto a warmed serving dish and serve at once on a bed of savory rice. Chutney goes well with this dish.

Cook's Notes

TIME
Preparation takes about 20 minutes, cooking about 20 minutes.

FREEZING
Open freeze the cooked meatballs, then pack in plastic bags or rigid containers. Seal, label and freeze for up to 2 months.

MICROWAVE
Follow step 1. In small casserole, cook onion, covered, on High until tender. Stir ingredients into ground beef mixture until mixed.

●300 calories per portion

Egg and Lemon Meatballs

SERVES 4
1½ lb lean ground beef
2 slices bread, crusts removed
1 large onion, grated
2 eggs, beaten
salt and pepper, to taste
2 cups water
½ cup lemon juice (see Cook's Tips)
1 tablespoon sugar
3 egg yolks
flour, for coating
paprika, to garnish

1 Put the bread in a small bowl, cover with cold water and leave to stand for about 10 minutes

2 Meanwhile, put the ground beef in a bowl. Add the onion and beaten eggs and stir well with a wooden spoon to mix and remove any lumps.

3 Squeeze the soaked bread with your hands to extract as much water as possible, then add to the beef mixture with salt and pepper to taste. Mix everything with your hands.

4 Divide the beef mixture into 20 portions and roll into balls with floured hands.

5 Pour the water into a saucepan. Add lemon juice, sugar and seasoning to taste and bring to a boil.

6 Add the meatballs to the pan a few at a time. Bring back to a boil, lower the heat, cover and simmer very gently for 40 minutes. Taste the cooking liquid and add more lemon juice or sugar if necessary.

7 Beat the egg yolks in a bowl. Remove the pan from the heat and, using a large metal spoon, very gradually trickle the hot liquid onto the egg yolks, beating all the time.

8 When most of the liquid from the pan has been added to the yolks, return the mixture to the pan and, off the heat, carefully turn the meatballs to coat them thoroughly in the sauce. Transfer the meatballs to warmed soup bowls, sprinkle with paprika and serve at once with plenty of mashed potatoes.

Cook's Notes

TIME
Preparation takes about 25 minutes. Cooking takes about 40 minutes, finishing the sauce about 5 minutes.

COOK'S TIPS
The average lemon contains about 2 tablespoons juice, so you will need about 4 lemons for this recipe.

The sauce should be sweet and sour. Adjust it accordingly, adding more lemon juice for extra sharpness or a pinch of sugar if it is too sour.

WATCHPOINTS
Add the hot liquid to the egg yolks very slowly or the mixture will curdle. If you need to reheat the dish once the egg yolks are incorporated, do so very gently, over very low heat, and do not allow to boil.

SERVING IDEAS
Serve the meatballs in soup bowls as there is a lot of sauce.

●595 calories per portion

Gloucester Cottage Pie

SERVES 4-6

1 lb lean ground beef
1 lb potatoes, peeled
1 tablespoon vegetable oil
1 onion, finely chopped
1 carrot, finely chopped
1 celery stalk, finely chopped
1 leek, finely chopped
2 tablespoons sweet brown chutney
  or relish
1¼ cups beef broth
1 cup finely diced cooked ham
  (optional)
2 tablespoons all-purpose flour
2 tablespoons tomato paste
3 tablespoons water
salt and pepper, to taste
½ cup shredded Double Gloucester
  cheese (see Variation)

1 Bring a saucepan of salted water to a boil, add the potatoes and cook for 10 minutes, until just tender. Drain and leave to cool.

2 Meanwhile, heat the oil in a saucepan, add the onion and cook gently for 5 minutes, until soft.

3 Add the carrot, celery and leek and continue cooking for about 3-4 minutes, stirring occasionally.

4 Add the ground beef and cook for 2-3 minutes, until the meat is evenly browned, stirring with a wooden spoon to remove any lumps. Drain off any excess fat from the pan, then stir in the chutney and broth. Cover and simmer gently for 30 minutes.

5 Preheat the oven to 350°.

6 Remove pan from the heat and stir in the ham, if using.

7 In a bowl, blend the flour with the tomato paste and water and stir into the pan. Return to the heat, bring to a boil, then lower the heat and simmer for 2 minutes, stirring. Season.

8 Transfer the beef mixture to a deep baking dish. Thinly slice the potatoes and arrange these neatly overlapping to cover the surface completely, then sprinkle with shredded cheese.

9 Cook for 20-30 minutes, or until the top is golden brown. Serve pie at once, straight from the dish.

Cook's Notes

TIME
The dish takes about 1 hour to prepare. Baking takes 20-30 minutes.

MICROWAVE
Follow step 1. In medium casserole, cook carrot and celery, covered, on High until very hot. Add beef and onion. Cover. Cook on High until beef is set and vegetables are tender, stirring occasionally. Drain. Stir in chutney and broth. Cover. Cook on High until hot. Cook on Medium to blend flavors. Follow steps 5-9.

VARIATION
Double Gloucester is a pungent English cheese. If unavailable, substitute Cheddar cheese.

•470 calories per portion

Meatball Casserole

SERVES 4

1½ lb lean ground beef
1 onion, grated
1 cup soft white bread crumbs
1 egg, beaten
2 tablespoons tomato paste
1 teaspoon Worcestershire sauce
salt and pepper, to taste
3 tablespoons all-purpose flour
3 tablespoons vegetable oil
1 onion, chopped
1 lb potatoes, cut into 1-inch chunks
3 carrots, sliced
2 cups beef broth
1 × 16 oz can tomatoes
3 zucchini, cut into ¾-inch
  pieces
½ teaspoon dried thyme
1 bay leaf

1 Put the ground beef in a bowl with the grated onion, bread crumbs, egg, tomato paste, Worcestershire sauce and salt and pepper to taste. Mix well until thoroughly blended, then divide the mixture into 20 pieces. Roll each piece into a ball with floured hands.

2 Spread the flour out on a flat plate and roll the meatballs in it until they are evenly coated, shaking off and reserving the excess flour.

3 Heat 2 tablespoons of the oil in a large heatproof Dutch oven. Add the meatballs a few at a time and cook over medium heat for 5-6 minutes, until well browned all over, turning frequently. Remove with a slotted spoon and drain on paper towels. Continue until all the meatballs are browned.

4 Heat the remaining oil in the pan, add onion, potatoes and carrots and cook for 4-5 minutes, stirring constantly. Stir in the reserved flour, then the broth and tomatoes with their juice. Bring to a boil, stirring and scraping any sediment off the base and sides of the pan. Add the zucchini, thyme, bay leaf and salt and pepper to taste, lower the heat,

Cook's Notes

TIME
Preparation takes about 45 minutes. Cooking takes about 40 minutes.

MICROWAVE
Follow step 1. In shallow baking dish, cook meatballs on High until firm, stirring occasionally. Drain. Set aside. In medium casserole, combine onion, potatoes and carrots. Cover. Cook on High until carrot is tender-crisp, stirring occasionally. Stir in flour, broth, tomatoes and juice, zucchini, thyme, bay leaf, seasoning. Cover. Cook on High until hot. Cook on Medium until tender, stirring occasionally. Add meatballs. Cover. Cook on High until hot.

WATCHPOINT
Be careful not to break up the meatballs when turning them in the sauce.

●590 calories per portion

cover and simmer for 15 minutes.
5 Add the meatballs to the pan and stir gently to cover them with sauce.

Cover and simmer for a further 25 minutes. Serve at once, straight from the Dutch oven.

Meatballs with Tomato Sauce

SERVES 6
1½ lb lean ground beef
1 small onion, chopped
3½ cups soft white bread crumbs
½ teaspoon dry mustard powder
½ teaspoon Italian seasoning
3 eggs, beaten
vegetable oil, for cooking

TOMATO SAUCE
2 tablespoons vegetable oil
1 large onion, chopped
1 clove garlic, crushed (optional)
3 bacon slices, cut into strips
1 × 16 oz can tomatoes
½ teaspoon Italian seasoning
⅔ cup beef broth
salt and pepper, to taste

1 To make the sauce, heat the oil in a saucepan, add the onion, garlic, if using, and bacon and cook gently for 5 minutes, until soft.
2 Add the tomatoes with their juice, herbs and broth. Season to taste, cover and simmer for 20 minutes.
3 Meanwhile, to make the meatballs, put the beef, onion, 1½ cups of the bread crumbs, mustard and the herbs in a bowl. Season and mix.
4 Beat eggs in a bowl, then stir in just enough to bind beef mixture. Mix thoroughly. Divide the mixture into 18 portions and, with floured hands, form into balls.
5 Spread the remaining bread crumbs out on a large flat plate. Dip the balls in remaining beaten egg, to coat, then roll them in the crumbs.
6 Preheat the oven to 225°.
7 Heat oil to a depth of ½ inch in a large skillet, add a few of the meatballs and cook for about 5 minutes, turning occasionally, until evenly browned and cooked through. Drain on paper towels, transfer to a warmed serving dish and keep warm in the oven while frying the remainder. Gently reheat the sauce.
8 Serve the meatballs at once, with the tomato sauce handed separately.

Cook's Notes

 TIME
Preparation and cooking takes 1 hour.

 MICROWAVE
In medium casserole cook onion, garlic and bacon on High until onion softens, stirring occasionally. Add tomatoes and juice, herbs, broth and seasoning. Cook, covered, on Medium-high until flavors blend, stirring occasionally. Follow steps 3-8.

SERVING IDEAS
Serve with plenty of mashed potatoes.

●555 calories per portion

Meatballs with Walnuts

SERVES 4-6

1½ lb lean ground beef
2 tablespoons vegetable or walnut oil (see Cook's Tip)
⅔ cup chopped walnuts
½ cup milk
2 slices whole wheat bread, crusts removed
1 egg, beaten
grated rind and juice of ½ lemon
salt and pepper, to taste
1 tablespoon margarine or butter
1 tablespoon all-purpose flour
1¼ cups beef broth
2 tablespoons heavy cream
walnut halves and lemon twists, to garnish

1 Heat the oil in a skillet, add the chopped walnuts and cook gently for 5 minutes, stirring often. Remove nuts from the pan with a slotted spoon and drain well on paper towels. Reserve oil in the skillet.

2 Transfer three-quarters of the nuts to a large bowl. Put the milk in a separate shallow bowl and add the bread. Press the bread down well with a fork to absorb the milk. Break up the soaked bread with the fork and add to the nuts.

3 Add the ground beef, egg and lemon rind and juice and stir very thoroughly to mix. Season to taste. Take heaped teaspoons of the mixture and roll into about 24 balls.

4 Melt the margarine in a large saucepan, sprinkle in the flour and stir over low heat for 1-2 minutes, until straw-colored. Gradually stir in the broth and simmer, stirring, until thick and smooth.

5 Add the meatballs to the saucepan and bring to a boil. Lower the heat, cover and simmer for 40 minutes.

6 Stir in the cream and remaining walnuts and heat through gently. Taste and adjust the seasoning, if necessary. Transfer to a warmed serving dish, garnish with walnut halves and serve at once.

Cook's Notes

TIME
Preparation takes about 25 minutes and cooking about 45 minutes.

MICROWAVE
Follow steps 1-3. In large casserole, melt butter on High. Stir in flour and broth. Cook on High until bubbly, stirring often. Add meatballs. Cook on High until hot. Stir. Cover. Cook on Medium until firm, stirring.

COOK'S TIP
Walnut oil is expensive but it is worth buying a small bottle or can. It can also be used in salad dressings.

●640 calories per portion

then add the green pepper and cook for a further 5 minutes or until the rice is tender. Drain.

5 Remove the meat mixture from the heat. Liberally grease a 5-cup heatproof bowl or pudding mold. Spoon a layer of rice into the mold, then a layer of meat mixture, then a layer of beans. Repeat these layers once more, then top with a final layer of rice. Cover the bowl with aluminum foil and place in a large saucepan. Pour in boiling water to come halfway up the sides of the bowl, cover and gently simmer the beef layer for 40 minutes.

6 Remove the bowl from the saucepan, using oven gloves or pot holders. Cool slightly, remove the foil and run a knife around the bowl. Place a warmed serving plate on top, securely hold both the bowl and plate, turn upside down with a slight shake and carefully turn out the beef layer.

7 Peel and slice the avocado. Top the beef layer with avocado slices and serve at once with tomato sauce.

Mexican Beef Layer

SERVES 4
½ lb lean ground beef
1 tablespoon vegetable oil
2 onions, finely chopped
4 slices bacon, finely
    chopped
1 clove garlic, crushed (optional)
1 bay leaf
2 teaspoons tomato paste
1 tablespoon tomato catsup
¼ cup golden raisins
1 tablespoon light brown sugar
½ teaspoon chili powder
⅔ cup broth
salt, to taste
1 cup Italian risotto rice
1 green pepper, seeded and finely
    chopped
1 x 17 oz can red kidney beans,
    drained
pepper, to taste

margarine, for greasing
1 small avocado, to garnish
1¼ cups tomato sauce, to serve

1 Heat the oil in a large saucepan, add the chopped onion and the chopped bacon and cook gently for 5 minutes, until the onion is soft and lightly colored. With a slotted spoon, transfer the onion and bacon to a plate and set aside.

2 Add the ground beef to the pan and cook over high heat for a few minutes, until the meat is evenly browned, stirring with a wooden spoon to remove any lumps.

3 Return the onion and bacon to the pan with the garlic, if using, the bay leaf, tomato paste, tomato catsup, sugar, chili powder and broth. Cover the pan, bring almost to a boil then lower heat and cook very gently for about 30 minutes, stirring occasionally.

4 Meanwhile, bring a large saucepan of salted water to a boil, add the rice and cook for 10 minutes,

Cook's Notes

TIME
Preparation takes about 30 minutes. Cooking the beef and rice takes about 30 minutes, layering about 5 minutes and steaming 40 minutes. Turning out the beef layer and garnishing with the avocado slices takes about 5 minutes.

MICROWAVE
In medium casserole, cook beef, onion and garlic on High until beef is set and onion is tender, stirring often. Add ingredients as step 3. Cover. Cook on Medium-high until flavors blend, stirring occasionally. Follow steps 4-7 as directed.

● 670 calories per portion

Quick Beef Curry

SERVES 4

1 lb lean ground beef
1 large onion, chopped
1 clove garlic, crushed
   (optional)
1 tablespoon curry powder (in
   strength to taste)
¼ teaspoon ground ginger
¼ teaspoon ground cumin
1 tart apple, pared and grated
¼ cup golden or seedless
   raisins
1 × 10½ oz can beef consommé
salt and pepper, to taste
1 cup quartered mushrooms

Cook's Notes

TIME
A quick-and-easy dish taking about 40 minutes to prepare and cook.

MICROWAVE
In medium casserole, cook beef, onion and garlic on High until meat is set, stirring occasionally. Stir in spices, apple, golden raisins, consommé, salt and pepper. Cook on High to boiling. Stir in mushrooms. Cover. Cook on Medium-high until flavors blend, stirring once.

●400 calories per portion

1 Place the beef, onion and garlic in a saucepan and cook over medium heat until the beef is well browned, stirring constantly with a wooden spoon to break up any lumps.
2 Stir in the spices and cook for 2 minutes, then stir in the apple, raisins and the beef consommé. Season with salt and pepper to taste.
3 Bring to a boil, then simmer gently for 5 minutes.
4 Stir in the mushrooms and simmer a further 10 minutes. Taste and adjust seasoning. Serve at once.

Surprise Meat Triangles

SERVES 4

¾ lb lean ground beef (see Buying Guide)
good pinch of cayenne
salt, to taste
¼ cup cheese spread or 8 individual wedge-shaped portions of cheese spread (see Buying Guide)
2 eggs
3 cups day-old bread crumbs
vegetable oil, for deep frying

1 Put the beef in a bowl and mix in the cayenne and salt to taste.
2 Divide into 8 portions and put on a clean board. Then, using a small spatula or your fingers, flatten each one into a triangular shape about 4 inches on each side.
3 Press a cheese portion into the center of each beef triangle. Mold and seal the beef evenly and completely around the cheese, being very careful to cover the corners. The edges must be well sealed or the cheese will leak out during cooking.
4 Beat the eggs in a shallow bowl and spread out the bread crumbs on a large flat plate. Dip each triangle into the egg, then into the bread crumbs, pressing firmly to coat evenly. Repeat a second time with each triangle.
5 Pour enough oil into a deep-fat fryer to come halfway up the sides of the triangles and heat to 350° or until a day-old bread cube will brown in 60 seconds.
6 Using a slotted spoon, lower half the triangles into the hot oil and deep-fry for about 7 minutes, until well browned.
7 Drain on paper towels and keep warm while cooking the second batch. Serve as soon as they are all cooked with lettuce, broiled whole tomatoes and sauté onion.

Cook's Notes

TIME
Total preparation and cooking time is 30-40 minutes from start to finish.

BUYING GUIDE
Buy very lean ground beef so that it does not shrink during cooking.

Processed cheese triangles are available in different flavors, individually wrapped in flat round boxes.

VARIATION
Instead of processed cheese portions, use small cubes of cheese and shape the beef into balls. Any soft melting cheese, such as mozzarella, would be suitable.

●385 calories per portion

Beef and Yorkshire Pudding

SERVES 4
3-3½ lb beef rib pot roast
salt and pepper, to taste
2 tablespoons beef dripping or shortening

YORKSHIRE PUDDING
2 eggs
1 cup milk
1 cup all-purpose flour
½ teaspoon each dried rosemary and basil

1 Preheat the oven to 400°.
2 Place the beef in a roasting pan. Season to taste with salt and pepper and dot with the dripping. Roast in the oven, basting occasionally, for 1¼ to 1½ hours, depending on whether you like your meat rare or well cooked.
3 Meanwhile, to make the Yorkshire pudding batter, place all the ingredients in an electric blender for 5-10 seconds, until smooth. Set aside to rest for 30 minutes. (If you are in a hurry, this resting time can be ignored.)
4 Spoon 2 tablespoons of the hot dripping from the roasting pan into the base of a warmed 8-inch baking pan. Pour the batter into the pan and bake in the center of the oven for 35 to 40 minutes, until it is well risen and golden brown.
5 Remove the meat from the oven and transfer to a warmed serving dish. Serve at once, carved into slices, with the Yorkshire pudding cut into wedges.

Cook's Notes

TIME
Preparation and cooking take 1 hour 20 minutes to 1 hour 35 minutes, depending how you like your meat.

BUYING GUIDE
Beef rib pot roast, is not a prime roasting cut, but can be successfully roasted provided the meat is well hung. Avoid bright red meat. This means it has been very recently cut and will tend to be tough.

SERVING IDEAS
Serve with roast potatoes and lightly cooked buttered cabbage. Make a gravy from the pan juices and beef broth and hand separately in a warmed gravy boat or pitcher.

DID YOU KNOW
Recipes for Yorkshire pudding have changed very little from when they were first written in the 19th century. In those days the pan was always placed under the spit-roasted meat to use all the dripping and juices that fell from the beef joint. Traditionally, in northern England, Yorkshire pudding was eaten on its own with gravy before the main course of meat, or sometimes at the end of the meal as a dessert, spread with homemade jam.

●885 calories per portion

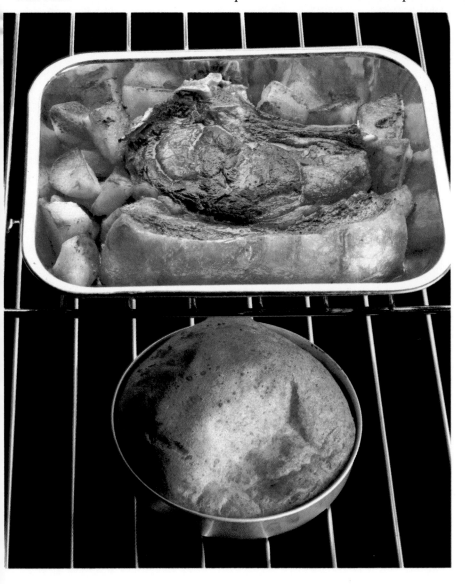

Gaelic Beef

SERVES 4-6
2½-3½ lb boneless rolled chuck or
    fillet, rolled and tied
6 tablespoons butter, softened
¼ cup all-purpose flour
1 tablespoon dry mustard
pepper, to taste
1¼ cups water
6-8 scallion tassels, to garnish
    (see Serving Ideas)

SCOTCH WHISKY GRAVY
2 tablespoons butter
1 bunch scallions, finely
    chopped
¼ cup all-purpose flour
3 tablespoons heavy cream
1-2 tablespoons Scotch whisky,
    to taste
1-2 teaspoons rich soy sauce
salt, to taste

1 Preheat the oven to 425°. Preheat the broiler to medium.
2 Weigh the beef and calculate the cooking time at 20 minutes per 1 lb, plus an extra 20 minutes.
3 Melt ¼ cup butter in a skillet, add the beef and cook quickly over high heat to brown on all sides. Remove, set aside on a plate to cool.
4 Line broiler with aluminum foil and sprinkle over the flour. Heat until flour is pale golden brown.
5 Mix the browned flour with the mustard and season with pepper. Spread the beef all over with the remaining butter, then dust with the seasoned flour, until evenly coated.
6 Place the beef on a rack in a roasting pan. Pour water into base of pan.
7 Roast in the oven for 20 minutes, then lower oven heat to 325° and cook for remaining time, basting occasionally with the pan juices, until the beef is tender and juices run clear when it is pierced with a skewer.
8 Transfer the beef to a warmed serving dish, remove the string, cover with aluminum foil and leave in a warm place.
9 Strain the juices from the roasting pan into a measuring cup and make up to 1¼ cups with water.
10 Melt the butter in a small saucepan, add the scallions and cook gently for 5 minutes, until soft and lightly colored. Sprinkle in the flour and cook for 1 further minute. Gradually blend in the meat juices and water. Bring to a boil and simmer for 2 minutes, stirring constantly. Remove from heat and stir in the cream. Add the Scotch and soy sauce to taste and season.
11 Carve the beef into thin slices, garnish with scallion tassels and hand the gravy in a gravy boat.

Cook's Notes

TIME
Preparation takes 30 minutes. Cooking in the oven takes 1¼-1½ hours and finishing takes about 10 minutes.

MICROWAVE
Follow steps 1-9. In small casserole, cook butter and onion on High until tender. Stir in flour and meat juices. Cook on High until thickened, stirring occasionally. Stir in cream. Blend in whisky, soy sauce, salt. Follow step 11.

COOK'S TIP
This time will give fairly rare beef. If you prefer more well-done meat, allow 25 minutes per 1 lb, plus an extra 25 minutes.

SERVING IDEAS
To make scallion tassels, slice off the roots and top portions. Make fine slashes at both ends and place in ice water until the ends curl as shown.

●865 calories per portion

Marinated Beef

SERVES 4-6
2 lb eye round roast or back of
   rib roast
1 tablespoon vegetable oil
⅔ cup beef broth
2 tablespoons all-purpose flour
tarragon sprigs, to garnish
   (optional)

MARINADE
⅔ cup dry red wine
¼ cup olive oil
1 onion, chopped
1 clove garlic, crushed (optional)
1 carrot, sliced
2 tablespoons finely chopped fresh
   tarragon, or ½ teaspoon dried
   tarragon
salt and pepper, to taste

1 Place beef in a bowl or Dutch oven just large enough to hold it comfortably. Combine all marinade ingredients and then pour over the beef. Cover and leave in a cool place for 8 hours or overnight, turning the beef occasionally in the marinade during this time.

2 Preheat the oven to 375°.

3 Remove beef from marinade and pat dry with paper towels. Reserve the marinade.

4 Brush the base of a roasting pan with 1 tablespoon oil. Place the beef in the pan, then roast for 1 hour, turning the beef halfway through the cooking time, until the juices run slightly pink when meat is pierced with a skewer (For well-done meat, roast for a further 15 minutes.)

5 Meanwhile, strain the marinade into a measuring cup (save the vegetables for soup) and make up to 1¼ cups with the beef broth.

6 Transfer the beef to a warmed serving dish and keep warm in the oven turned to lowest setting. Drain all but 2 tablespoons of the cooking juices from the roasting pan, then place the pan on top of the stove and sprinkle in the flour. Stir for 1-2 minutes over low heat, then blend in the marinade. Bring to a boil, stirring, until thick and smooth. Taste and adjust seasoning.

7 Carve the beef into neat thick slices and spoon over a little of the sauce. Garnish with tarragon sprigs, if liked. Pour the remaining sauce into a warmed pitcher and hand separately with the beef.

Cook's Notes

TIME
Allow 8 hours marinating, then preparation takes about 10 minutes and cooking 1 hour.

SERVING IDEAS
Serve the beef hot with buttered unpeeled new potatoes and green beans.

MICROWAVE
Follow steps 1-5. Transfer beef to warmed dish and keep warm. Place 2 tablespoons cooking juices in small casserole. Stir in flour and marinade. Cook on High until thickened, stirring occasionally. Follow step 7.

•600 calories per portion

Roast Beef with Horseradish

SERVES 6
3-3½ lb eye round roast or sirloin tip roast
⅔ cup plain yogurt
2 teaspoons red wine vinegar
2 tablespoons creamed horseradish
salt and pepper, to taste
2½ cups hot beef broth

BEURRE MANIÉ (kneaded butter)
1 tablespoon all-purpose flour
1 tablespoon butter

1 Put the beef into a roasting pan. Mix together the yogurt, wine vinegar and horseradish in a bowl and season with salt and pepper.
2 Spread the horseradish mixture over the beef, covering the surface completely. Marinate in a cool place for 2 hours (see Cook's Tips).
3 Preheat the oven to 425°.
4 Put the roasting pan into the oven and cook the beef for 55-60 minutes (see Cook's Tips).
5 Lower oven to 225°. Transfer the beef to a warmed serving platter. Carve the beef into neat slices and keep hot in the oven.
6 To make the beurre manié, blend the flour and butter together with a spatula to make a paste, then cut the paste into pea-sized pieces.
7 Scrape any burnt pieces from the roasting pan and discard. Put the pan on top of the stove and pour in the broth, then add pieces of beurre manié, a few at a time, and cook over medium heat, stirring until the sauce thickens. Season to taste, then strain the sauce into a warmed sauce boat or pitcher.
8 Pour a little sauce over the beef and serve with roast potatoes, a green vegetable and carrots, with the remaining sauce handed separately.

Rolled Beef and Potato Salad

SERVES 4

8 slices cooked roast beef, total
  weight about ¾ lb (see Buying
  Guide)
1 lb new potatoes, unpeeled
salt, to taste
1 red pepper, halved crosswise and
  seeded
½ large bunch watercress, trimmed
lettuce leaves, to garnish

DRESSING

½ cup mayonnaise
¼ cup plain yogurt
4½ teaspoons horseradish sauce
pepper, to taste

1 Bring the potatoes to a boil in salted water, lower the heat and cook for 15-20 minutes, until they are tender.

2 Meanwhile, bring a saucepan of water just to a boil. Add 1 pepper half and boil gently for 8 minutes, until tender. Drain, rinse with cold water and drain again. Pat dry with paper towels and dice. Slice remaining pepper half very thinly and reserve for the garnish.

3 Reserve half the watercress for garnish; finely chop the remainder.

4 Combine the dressing ingredients in a bowl and season to taste.

5 Drain and rinse the cooked potatoes under cold running water, then drain again. Peel off the skins, then dice the potatoes into small pieces. Put half the diced potato into a bowl with the diced red pepper and season. Put the remaining potato into another bowl with the chopped watercress and season with salt and pepper.

6 Add half the dressing to each bowl and stir gently to mix. Cover and chill the potato salads for at least 30 minutes.

7 Lay 4 of the beef slices on a board; spoon a quarter of the watercress and potato mixture onto each slice and roll up. Lay the remaining beef slices on the board, spoon a quarter

Cook's Notes

TIME
Preparation, including filling the rolls, takes about 1 hour. Allow 30 minutes chilling time for potato salads.

BUYING GUIDE
Buy the sliced roast beef from the delicatessen counter of a supermarket. The slices should not be too thin, or they will fall apart when rolled.

●460 calories per portion

of the red pepper and potato mixture onto each slice and roll up.

8 Arrange one of each type of filled beef rolls alternately on a large platter and garnish well with lettuce and extra pepper rings and watercress sprigs, if desired. Serve at once, while chilled as a summer lunch or part of a buffet.

Spiced Roast Rib of Beef

SERVES 4-6
4-4½ lb standing rib roast
¼ cup butter
1 clove garlic, crushed (optional)
2 teaspoons mustard
1 teaspoon ground allspice
1 tablespoon all-purpose flour
watercress sprigs, to garnish

GRAVY
¼ cup all-purpose flour
1¼ cups beef broth
1 tablespoon red wine vinegar or dry red wine
salt and pepper, to taste

1 Preheat the oven to 425°.

2 Weigh the joint and calculate the cooking time, allowing 20 minutes per 1 lb (see Cook's Tip). Place beef on a rack in a roasting pan. Set aside while making the topping.

3 Cream together the butter, garlic, if using, mustard and allspice, then beat in the flour. Spread the mixture evenly all over the meat.

4 Roast for 20 minutes, then lower the oven temperature to 375°, and start the cooking time from then.

5 Transfer the meat to a warmed serving dish and keep warm in the oven turned to its lowest setting.

6 To make the gravy pour off excess fat from the roasting pan and stir in the flour. Place on top of the stove, pour in the broth and bring slowly to a boil, stirring constantly and scraping the sediment from the bottom. Add vinegar and simmer for a further 2-3 minutes. Season to taste, then pour into a warmed gravy boat.

7 Garnish the beef with watercress sprigs and serve at once with the gravy handed separately.

Cook's Notes

TIME
Preparation takes about 10 minutes, cooking takes about 1¾-2 hours.

COOK'S TIP
This cooking time will give a medium-rare result. For a well-done roast, add 15 minutes to total time.

SERVING IDEAS
Serve the beef with roast potatoes, horse-radish sauce, glazed carrots and a seasonal green vegetable like broccoli. This roast beef is equally delicious served cold with a salad.

●985 calories per portion

Summer Beef Salad

SERVES 4
1½-2 lb beef for roasting
7 tablespoons vegetable oil
⅔ cup dry white wine
1 teaspoon mild mustard
1 teaspoon dried thyme
1 tablespoon lemon juice
1 clove garlic, crushed (optional)
salt and pepper, to taste
1 small onion, finely sliced

SALAD
2 potatoes, peeled
¼ lb French-style green beans,
   fresh or frozen
2 carrots, grated
2 tomatoes, quartered

GARNISH
8-10 ripe olives
1 tablespoon chopped fresh parsley

1 Preheat the oven to 350°.
2 Wrap the beef in aluminum foil and place in a roasting pan. Roast in the oven for about 1 hour (see Cook's Tips). Remove from the oven and leave the beef to cool for about 45 minutes, still wrapped in foil.
3 To make the marinade, put the oil, wine, mustard, thyme, lemon juice and garlic, if using, in a bowl or in the goblet of a blender. Season and beat well with a fork, or process in the blender for 30 seconds.
4 Slice the cooled beef into even, neat slices and arrange them in a shallow dish. Arrange the onion slices on top of the beef and pour over the marinade. Cover the dish of beef with plastic wrap and refrigerate for at least 5-6 hours or overnight.
5 To make the salad, cook the potatoes in boiling salted water for 15-20 minutes or until just tender. Drain, cool slightly and cut into bite-sized cubes. Meanwhile, cook the beans in boiling salted water for 5-10 minutes or until just tender. Drain well and mix with the potatoes in a bowl. While the vegetables are still

warm, pour 2 tablespoons of the marinade from the beef over and gently turn them with a fork, without breaking, to coat thoroughly with the marinade. Cover and chill for 1 hour.
6 When ready to serve, mix the grated carrots and the tomatoes with the potatoes and beans. Remove the meat slices from the marinade, draining off any excess marinade from the slices. Remove the onions from the marinade and mix them into the vegetables.
7 Pile the vegetable salad into the center of a serving platter and arrange the marinated beef slices around it. Garnish the platter with ripe olives and chopped parsley. Serve at once.

Cook's Notes

TIME
Cooking the beef takes about 1 hour. Allow 5-6 hours or overnight for marinating. Preparing the salad takes about 30 minutes. Allow 1 hour for chilling the salad.

COOK'S TIPS
The meat will be just pink after 1 hour's cooking. Cook for 50 minutes for rare beef, and for 1¼ hours if you like it well done.

● 440 calories per portion

Beet and Apple Purée

SERVES 6
1 lb cooked beets, peeled and diced
2 tablespoons butter
1 large onion, finely chopped
1 lb tart apples, pared, cored
  and sliced
2 tablespoons water
2 tablespoons light brown
  sugar
½ teaspoon ground nutmeg
½ teaspoon ground cloves
salt and pepper, to taste

TO FINISH
⅔ cup sour cream
2 tablespoons snipped chives

1 Melt the butter in a large saucepan, add the onion and cook gently for about 5 minutes, until soft.
2 Add the beets and apple and continue to cook gently for a further 10 minutes. Stir in the water, sugar, spices and season to taste. Cover the pan and simmer gently for 40 minutes until the apple is pulpy.
3 Press through a strainer, or leave to cool slightly, then work in a blender until smooth.
4 Transfer to a large bowl, leave to cool completely, then cover and chill for at least 2 hours.
5 To serve, divide the purée between 6 ramekin dishes, smooth the surface, then top with sour cream and sprinkle with chives. Serve.

Cook's Notes

TIME
15 minutes preparation; about 1 hour cooking and at least 2 hours chilling.

SERVING IDEAS
Serve with hot garlic bread, toast or crackers as an unusual appetizer to a dinner party.

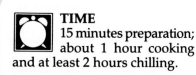

MICROWAVE
In medium casserole, cook butter, onion, beets and apple, covered, on High until apple and onion are tender, stirring once or twice. Add water, sugar, spices, seasoning. Cover. Cook on Medium until apple is pulpy, stirring occasionally.

FREEZING
Pour the cold purée into a rigid container, seal, label and freeze for up to 3 months. To serve, thaw in the covered container in the refrigerator for 6-8 hours. Beat before putting into ramekins.

●165 calories per portion

Beet and Celery Salad

SERVES 4
1 lb cooked beets (see Buying Guide)
4 celery stalks
1 hard-boiled egg, quartered

DRESSING
6 tablespoons olive oil
2 tablespoons wine vinegar
½ teaspoon sugar
3 tablespoons country-Dijon mustard
1 tablespoon chopped fresh parsley
salt and pepper, to taste
1 tablespoon light cream

1 Peel the beets and cut into sticks, about 1½-inches long and ¼-inch wide. Place in a salad bowl or on a serving plate.

Cook's Notes

TIME
This salad only takes 20 minutes preparation.

VARIATION
The parsley can be replaced by another fresh herb – try tarragon or dill.

COOK'S TIP
This salad may be prepared in advance, but do not mix until just before serving, or beets will run.

BUYING GUIDE
Buy ready-cooked beets from supermarkets. Alternatively, cook raw beets. Cut off the leaves ½-inch from their base and do not trim or cut into the root. Rinse and cook in lightly salted boiling water for 1-2 hours, or wrap in foil and bake 1-2 hours in a 325° oven. Rub off skins while the beets are still warm.

● 285 calories per portion

2 Cut the celery stalks diagonally into ¼-inch thick slices and reserve them separately.
3 To make the dressing, put the oil, vinegar, sugar, mustard and parsley in a screw-top jar, add salt and pepper to taste and shake well to mix.

Add the cream to the jar and stir the dressing thoroughly.
4 Add the celery to the beets and fold in gently. Pour the dressing over (see Cook's Tip).
5 Arrange the egg in the center of the salad and serve at once.

and salt and pepper to taste.

4 Roll out half the dough on a lightly floured surface and use to line a shallow 8-inch square pan. Roll out the remaining dough into a square slightly larger than the top of the pan and set aside.

5 Spread the filling over the dough in the pan. Dampen the edges of the dough with water, then lay the reserved dough square over the top. Press it onto the side of the dough lining about the level of the filling, then trim the dough level with the top of the pan.

6 Brush with cold water, sprinkle lightly with salt, then make a hole in the top for the steam to escape. Bake just above the center of the oven for 30-35 minutes or until crisp.

7 Serve hot, warm or cold.

Cook's Notes

TIME
This unusual pastry dish takes about 10 minutes to prepare and 30-35 minutes to bake.

BUYING GUIDE
Bottled pickled beets can be used instead of the canned julienne beets. Drain them well and omit the sweet relish.

VARIATIONS
Make the dough and filling into 6-8 slices. Use any well-flavored cheese you have in the pantry.

FREEZING
When cold, cut into slices and wrap individually in plastic wrap, then in foil. Freeze for up to 6 weeks. To serve, thaw at room temperature for 2-3 hours. If liked, heat through for 15 minutes in the oven preheated to 375°.

● 605 calories per portion

Beet and Cheese Bars

SERVES 4-6
1 package (10 oz) pie crust mix
water, to mix

FILLING
½ lb Cheddar cheese, shredded (see Variations)
2 × 8¼ oz cans julienne beets, drained
1 small onion, finely grated
1½ teaspoons Country-Dijon mustard
3 tablespoons mayonnaise
½ tablespoon sweet relish
salt and pepper, to mix

1 Prepare the pie crust dough according to package directions. Wrap in plastic wrap and chill for at least 30 minutes.

2 Preheat the oven to 400°.

3 Meanwhile, to make the filling, mix together the cheese, beets, onion, mustard, mayonnaise, relish

Beet in Horseradish Sauce

SERVES 4

4 cooked beets (total weight about 1½ lb), peeled and sliced under running water
2 tablespoons margarine or butter
1 bay leaf
1 onion, finely chopped
¼ cup all-purpose flour
1¼ cups milk
1½ tablespoons grated horseradish (see Buying Guide)
salt and pepper, to taste

1 Preheat the oven to 350°.
2 Arrange the beet slices in a shallow baking dish.
3 Melt the margarine in a saucepan, add the bay leaf and onion and cook gently for 5 minutes, until the onion is soft and translucent.

4 Sprinkle in the flour and stir over low heat for 2 minutes, until straw-colored. Remove from the heat and gradually stir in the milk.
5 Return to the heat and simmer, stirring, until thick and smooth. Add the horseradish and season with salt and pepper to taste.

6 Remove the sauce from the heat and discard the bay leaf. Work the sauce in a blender until smooth, then pour over the beets. Cover with a lid or aluminum foil and bake in the oven for 20 minutes, until the beets are heated through. Serve the beets hot, straight from the dish.

Cook's Notes

TIME
Preparation and cooking take about 35 minutes in all.

MICROWAVE
Follow step 2. In medium casserole cook bay leaf, onion and margarine, covered, on High until tender. Stir in flour and milk. Cook on Medium-high until thick, stirring occasionally. Stir in horseradish and seasoning. Discard bay leaf. Blend sauce until smooth. Pour over beets. Cover. Cook on Medium-high until heated through.

BUYING GUIDE
If fresh or bottled grated horseradish is not available, use 1½ tablespoons horseradish sauce.

●190 calories per portion

Jellied Beet Ring

SERVES 6-8
¾ lb cooked beets, cut
   into matchstick strips
1 × 3 oz package black cherry
   gelatin
⅔ cup boiling water
⅔ cup cold water
¼ cup red wine vinegar
salt and pepper, to taste
2 tablespoons snipped chives
mustard greens and garden cress,
   to garnish

SAVORY EGGS
4 hard-boiled eggs, chopped
5 tablespoons mayonnaise
2 tablespoons plain yogurt
4½ teaspoons horseradish sauce

1 Rinse out a 2½ cup-ring mold and refrigerate (see Microwave).
2 Dissolve the gelatin in a bowl with the boiling water. Stir about 2 minutes until completely dissolved, then stir in the cold water and vinegar. Season to taste.
3 Refrigerate the gelatin until thickened but not set.
4 Fold the beets and chives into thickened gelatin and spoon the gelatin into the chilled mold. Refrigerate for about 2 hours, until firm.
5 Meanwhile, to make the savory eggs, blend the mayonnaise, yogurt, and horseradish sauce together in a bowl. Fold in the chopped eggs and season to taste. Cover with plastic wrap and refrigerate.
6 About 30 minutes before serving, unmold the gelatin, ease the edges away from sides of the mold with your fingertips. Dip the mold into a bowl of hand-hot water for 1-2 seconds, then invert a dampened plate on top. Holding both mold and plate firmly, invert, giving a sharp shake halfway around. Lift off mold.
7 Fill the center with the savory eggs. Garnish with the mustard greens and garden cress and serve.

Cook's Notes

TIME
Preparation takes 25 minutes, plus cooling time and 2 hours to set.

VARIATIONS
The cooked beets may be replaced by a 1¼ lb jar of sliced pickled beets, in which case only use 2 tablespoons vinegar or the gelatin will tend to taste too sour. Blackberry and apple or a raspberry gelatin can be used in place of black cherry.

MICROWAVE
Follow step 1. In small bowl, cook gelatin on High until hot. Stir until melted. Stir in water and seasoning. Follow steps 3-7.

●220 calories per portion

Orange and Beet Salad

SERVES 4

4 cooked beets, peeled and sliced
2 oranges, peeled with any juice
   reserved
1 lettuce, leaves separated
2 large tomatoes, sliced
3-4 teaspoons finely chopped
   walnuts

DRESSING

1 teaspoon finely chopped onion
1 teaspoon snipped chives
salt, to taste
½ teaspoon mustard
good pinch of sugar
pepper, to taste
1 tablespoon red wine vinegar
   (see Variation)

3 tablespoons olive or vegetable oil
dash of Worcestershire sauce

1 Cut the orange horizontally into thin slices and set aside.
2 Arrange the lettuce leaves on a salad platter.
3 Arrange the orange and beet slices alternately in a ring on top of the lettuce. Arrange overlapping slices of tomato in the center of the dish and sprinkle with walnuts.
4 To make the dressing, put the reserved orange juice from the peeled oranges in a bowl. Add the onion and chives to the bowl, together with the salt, mustard and sugar and pepper to taste. Mix well together with a fork. Add the vinegar, oil and Worcestershire sauce and beat together until the dressing is well blended.
5 Spoon the prepared dressing over the salad and serve at once.

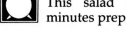

Cook's Notes

TIME
This salad takes 20 minutes preparation.

COOK'S TIP
Do not prepare too soon in advance or the beets may discolor the oranges.

SERVING IDEAS
Serve as a side salad with broiled fish or poultry, or as part of a buffet.

VARIATION
Use an herb-flavored vinegar, such as tarragon or mint vinegar.

●150 calories per portion

Red Cabbage with Beets

SERVES 6
1 lb red cabbage, shredded
   (see Preparation)
2 large cooked beets, sliced
salt to taste
2 tablespoons margarine
1 onion, sliced
1¼ cups chicken broth
2-3 tablespoons lemon juice
2 cloves
1 bay leaf
pepper, to taste
2 tablespoons butter, softened
1 cup pared and grated tart apples
1-2 tablespoons light brown
   sugar

1 Preheat the oven to 225°.
2 Bring a large saucepan of salted water to a boil, add the cabbage, bring back to a boil, then blanch for 2 minutes. Drain well.
3 Melt the margarine in the rinsed-out pan, add the onion and cook gently for 5 minutes, until soft and lightly colored. Stir in the cabbage, broth and 1 tablespoon lemon juice, then add the cloves, bay leaf and seasoning to taste.
4 Bring to a boil, then lower the heat slightly, cover and simmer gently for 1 hour. Add the cooked, sliced beets and cook for a further 10 minutes.
5 Drain the cabbage mixture, reserving the broth. Discard the cloves and bay leaf. Put the vegetables into a serving dish and gently mix in the butter. Taste and adjust seasoning, cover and keep hot in the oven.
6 Pour about ⅔ cup of the reserved broth into the rinsed-out pan, then add the grated apple and the remaining lemon juice. Cover and cook over moderate heat for about 10 minutes, until the apple is tender, then stir in the brown sugar and salt and pepper to taste.
7 Pour the sauce over the cabbage mixture and stir in gently until thoroughly combined. Serve at once (see Serving Ideas).

Cook's Notes

TIME
25 minutes preparation and about 1¼ hours cooking time.

PREPARATION
A food processor with a shredding disk quickly prepares the cabbage, but if slicing by hand, wear rubber gloves because the cabbage juices will temporarily stain the skin red.

SERVING IDEAS
Try topping the tossed dish with sour cream or yogurt. The hot cabbage is especially good with boiled ham, or with roast pork or game. If you are serving the cabbage with game, garnish with cooked chestnuts.

●105 calories per portion

Sweet and Sour Beets

SERVES 4-6
1½ lb uncooked beets, washed (see
    Watchpoint and Variation)
salt, to taste

SAUCE
2 tablespoons margarine or
    butter
1 tablespoon vegetable oil
1 onion, chopped
grated rind and juice of
    1 orange
2 tablespoons honey
1 tablespoon wine vinegar
pinch of ground cardamon
2 teaspoons cornstarch
1 tablespoon water
2 teaspoons soy sauce
1 teaspoon snipped chives

1 Bring a large pan of salted water to a boil. Lower the beets into the pan and simmer for about 1½-2 hours, until tender.

2 Drain the beets, reserving 2 tablespoons of the cooking liquid. Cut away the top and bottom and peel off the skin. Dice the flesh.

3 To make the sauce, heat the margarine and oil in a large saucepan, add the onion and cook gently for 5 minutes, until soft and lightly colored. Add the orange rind and juice, honey, wine vinegar and the ground cardamon.

4 Blend the cornstarch with the water and soy sauce and stir in with the reserved beet juice. Simmer gently for 2 minutes, stirring constantly until thick and smooth.

5 Add the diced beets and fold in gently. Transfer the mixture to a warmed serving dish and serve at once with roast or broiled meat, or with cold meats and salad.

Cook's Notes

TIME
This dish takes 2-2½ hours to make.

WATCHPOINT
Rinse the beets carefully under cold, running water. Do not scrub, bruise or pierce the skin of the beets, because this will cause the red juice to escape and "bleed" into the cooking water.

VARIATION
Beets can also be baked in the oven, if you prefer. Place in a roasting pan and bake for 1½-2 hours in an oven preheated to 350°.

●200 calories per portion

BELGIUM

Sometimes called the "Belgian bouillabaisse," Waterzootje is a creamy combination of fish and vegetables. Although fairly simple to make, it is delicious enough to form the centerpiece of a dinner party.

Although Waterzootje, a deliciously creamy fish soup, is famous as a classic Belgian dish, it is in fact a specialty of Flanders in the North of the country. Flemish cooking is based on the rich abundance of excellent raw materials, ranging from superb vegetables harvested around the town of Malines to fish and shellfish fresh from the North Sea.

Although deceptively simple—the high-quality ingredients do not need great embellishment—all great Flemish dishes have many subtle touches. Waterzootje is no exception—the combination of herbs and the mixture of egg yolks and cream enhance, rather than mask, the fresh vegetables and fish.

It is best to buy fresh, whole fish when making Waterzootje so that you can use the bones, skin and trimmings to make the stock. If you prefer not to prepare the fish yourself, ask at the fish counter at the supermarket for trimmings. If necessary, you can use frozen fish, but you will still need spare fish trimmings for the stock.

Waterzootje takes only about an hour to prepare and cook and is very simple to make as long as care is taken in all stages of cooking. The fish must be cut into equal-sized pieces so that it will all be cooked within the same time. Bring the water to the lowest possible simmering point—there should hardly be a tremor on the surface. If you allow the water to boil, the fish will be overcooked, tasteless and tough. Keep an eye on the cooking time—any longer than five minutes will spoil the fish.

Take care also when adding the egg and cream mixture to the soup. It is essential to blend in a ladle of hot soup; adding the egg yolks and cream directly to the hot liquid could cause the yolks to curdle.

Waterzootje should be served as a main course—it is far too filling to eat as an appetizer! Serve with hot French bread and butter, accompanied, if you like, with a dish of new potatoes, garnished with fresh parsley. No other vegetable is needed, except perhaps a simple green salad. To drink, either serve a light European—Belgian, if possible—beer, or a light, dry white wine such as a Moselle from Germany.

Waterzootje

SERVES 8
4-4½ lb snapper, flounder or perch cleaned, filleted and skinned, trimmings reserved
3 onions, sliced
3 cloves garlic (optional)
2 cups medium-dry white wine
juice of 1 lemon
thyme sprig
2 sage leaves, or pinch of dried sage
2 bay leaves
6 parsley sprigs
salt and pepper, to taste
¼ cup butter
1 lb leeks, chopped
1 small bunch celery, chopped
4 tablespoons chopped fresh parsley

TO SERVE
2 egg yolks, beaten
¼ cup light cream
2 tablespoons snipped chives
4 extra tablespoons light cream (optional)

1 Put the fish heads, tails, bones and trimmings in a very large saucepan with the onions, garlic, if using, wine, lemon juice, thyme, sage, bay leaves, parsley sprigs and salt and pepper to taste.

2 Pour in about 7 cups cold water to cover. Bring to a boil, then lower the heat, cover and simmer gently for 30 minutes.

3 Meanwhile, melt the butter in a large saucepan, add the leeks, celery and chopped parsley and cook gently, stirring from time to time, for about 5 minutes. Season to taste with salt and pepper. Pour in about 7 cups cold water to cover. Bring to a boil, then lower the heat, cover and simmer very gently for about 30 minutes, until the vegetables are tender but firm.

4 Meanwhile, pat the fish fillets dry with paper towels. Using a very sharp knife, cut them into equal-sized 1-1½-inch pieces.

5 Strain and measure the fish broth and, if necessary, boil rapidly to reduce to 6 cups. Then, strain the vegetables and measure 6 cups of the broth. Pour both of the broths into a very large saucepan or fish kettle and add the cooked vegetables. Taste and adjust the seasoning if necessary.

6 Bring the contents of the pan to a boil, then lower the heat to the very lowest simmering point. Gently lower the fish pieces into the pan, cover and simmer for no longer than 5 minutes, until the fish is just cooked. Be careful not to have the broth over too high of a setting or the fish will be overcooked. Remove at once from the heat.

7 In a warmed soup tureen or large bowl, combine the egg yolks with ¼ cup cream and the chives.

8 Thoroughly blend 1 ladle of hot soup with egg yolk mixture, then very carefully pour in the rest of the soup, making sure that the fish pieces do not break up. Serve at once in warmed soup bowls, with a spoonful of cream swirled on the top of each, if liked.

●355 calories per portion

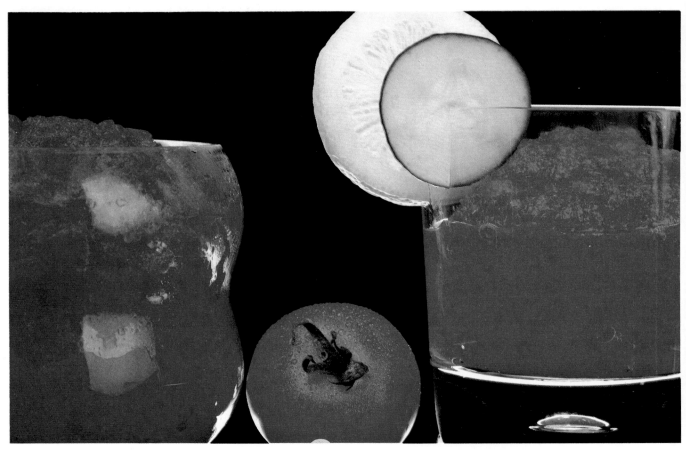

Iced Tomato Cocktail

SERVES 6
3 × 6 oz cans tomato juice
few drops of Worcestershire sauce
1 tablespoon medium-dry sherry
few drops of hot pepper sauce
  (optional)
celery salt, to taste
pepper, to taste
lemon and cucumber slices, to
  garnish

1 Put the tomato juice in the goblet of a blender, together with the Worcestershire sauce, sherry, hot pepper sauce, if using, celery salt and pepper to taste. Blend until all the ingredients are well combined. Alternatively, mix well together with a wire whisk.
2 Pour into a rigid container or freezer trays and freeze for 2 hours, until the mixture is firm around the sides (see Cook's Tip).
3 Remove the container from the freezer and beat the icy mixture with a whisk or fork until evenly blended. Return to the freezer for a further 3-4 hours or until the tomato ice is firmly frozen.
4 About 30 minutes before serving the cocktail, transfer the frozen mixture to the refrigerator to allow it to soften slightly.
5 Spoon the mixture into individual glasses and garnish with a slice each of lemon and cucumber.

Cook's Notes

 TIME
Preparation 5-10 minutes, freezing 5-6 hours.

COOK'S TIP
If you are using the freezer compartment of the refrigerator, turn it to its coldest setting 1 hour before making the cocktail and remember to turn it back to its original setting when you have finished making the cocktails.

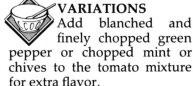 **VARIATIONS**
Add blanched and finely chopped green pepper or chopped mint or chives to the tomato mixture for extra flavor.

SERVING IDEAS
Serve as a refreshing appetizer before a meal, providing spoons.

●20 calories per portion

Irish Coffee

SERVES 4
2½ cups hot, strong black coffee
4 teaspoons sugar, or to taste
½ cup Irish whiskey
⅔ cup heavy cream, very lightly
whipped and chilled

1 Rinse out four 1-cup heat-proof stem goblets with hot water. Dry.
2 Put 1 teaspoon sugar into each goblet, then add the whiskey, dividing it equally between the goblets. Pour in the coffee, leaving room for the cream and stir well, adding more sugar, if liked.
3 Leave for a few seconds until settled, then add the cream. Serve.

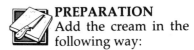

Cook's Notes

TIME
Preparation will take about 20 minutes, including making the coffee and whipping the cream.

COOK'S TIP
Make "real" coffee, from ground beans, for this recipe; instant coffee does not give the best result.

WATCHPOINT
If the cream is added too soon, or poured too quickly, it will not float and you will lose the contrast of chilled white cream and hot black coffee.

PREPARATION
Add the cream in the following way:

Hold a metal teaspoon, curved side up, across the rim of the goblet so that its tip just touches the coffee. Pour the cream very slowly over the back of the spoon so that it floats.

●225 calories per drink

Kid's Cooler

SERVES 4
12 ice cubes
1⅓ cups unsweetened
**   pineapple juice, chilled**
few drops of fresh lime juice
1⅓ cups unsweetened orange
**   juice, chilled**
2 tablespoons grenadine

TO GARNISH (OPTIONAL)
½ slice fresh pineapple with skin,
**   or 4 canned pineapple pieces,**
**   drained**
2 slices lime
2 small slices orange
8 maraschino or candied cherries

1 To prepare the garnish, if using,
cut the pineapple slice into quarters
to make 4 triangular wedges. Cut
each slice of citrus fruit into halves.
On each of 4 wooden cocktail sticks,
spear 1 cherry followed by 1 piece
each of lime, pineapple and orange,
then another cherry.
2 Put the 3 ice cubes into the bottom
of each of 4 highball glasses or tall
tumblers. Pour ⅓ cup pineapple
juice into each glass, add a squeeze
of lime, then ⅓ cup orange juice.
3 Pour a thin stream of grenadine,
straight from the bottle, in a circle
around the edge of each drink.
4 Garnish the drinks with the
prepared fruits, by balancing a
wooden cocktail stick across the top
of each glass. Put 1-2 long straws
into each drink and serve at once.

Cook's Notes

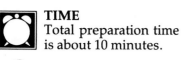 **TIME**
Total preparation time
is about 10 minutes.

BUYING GUIDE
Grenadine is a bright
red, sweet syrup,
flavored with pomegranate
juice. It is used to color, flavor
and sweeten some potent
cocktails, notably a Tequila
Sunrise. The bottle has a special top so you can pour the
syrup straight into the drinks.

For children, buy non-
alcoholic grenadine.

VARIATION
For an adult Kooler
with a kick, replace
some or all of the pineapple
juice with a colorless spirit
such as gin or vodka.

●90 calories per drink

Lemon and Lime Barley Water

MAKES ABOUT 4 CUPS
⅔ cup pearl barley
thinly pared rind and juice
of 1 small lemon and 1 small
lime
6 tablespoons sugar
5 cups boiling water

1 Put the barley into a heavy-bottomed saucepan and cover with cold water. Bring to a boil and simmer for 10 minutes, then strain off the liquid. Rinse the barley under cold running water and drain well.
2 Put the barley into a large heat-proof pitcher together with rind and 5 tablespoons sugar. Pour over the boiling water, cover and leave for 1-1½ hours, until cold.
3 Uncover and then stir in the fruit juice and more sugar, if liked. Strain the liquid into a clean pitcher and discard the barley (see Cook's Tips).
4 Serve the barley water at once (see Serving Ideas) or cover with plastic wrap and keep in the refrigerator and use within 2 days.

Cook's Notes

TIME
20 minutes preparation, plus cooling time.

VARIATIONS
Use oranges or limes or lemons on their own if preferred.

COOK'S TIPS
The barley will swell as it absorbs some of the water, so there will be less liquid than at start of soaking.
A cloudy layer will form at the bottom of the pitcher if the barley water is left to stand; in which case, stir thoroughly or beat before serving.

SERVING IDEAS
Serve in 4 tumblers, with plenty of ice; add 2 straws to each glass and decorate with thin slices of lemon or lime.

DID YOU KNOW
Barley water has been valued for its soothing properties and served as a drink for hundreds of years. In the Middle Ages it was often a popular custom to flavor it with licorice.
For a licorice flavor, break ¼ lb licorice sticks (available from health food shops) into small pieces and add to the barley with the rind and the sugar in step 2. (The boiling water melts the licorice.) Add the lemon and lime juice in step 3.

●85 calories per drink

Malted Milkshakes

SERVES 4
8 ice cubes, crushed
1-pint block vanilla ice cream,
    cut into cubes
3 tablespoons cocoa, sifted
2 teaspoons light brown sugar
1¼ cups milk
3 tablespoons malt extract (see
    Buying Guide)

TO FINISH (OPTIONAL)
4 scoops vanilla ice cream
chocolate flakes

1 Put 4 glass tumblers into the refrigerator to chill for 30 minutes.
2 Put half the ice and half the ice cream into a blender with half of the cocoa, sugar, milk and malt. Blend for 2 minutes, until frothy, resting the motor after 1 minute.
3 Pour into 2 of the chilled tumblers. Top each drink with a scoop of ice cream and chocolate flake, if liked. Serve at once.
4 Use the remaining ice, ice cream, cocoa, sugar, milk and malt to make 2 more milk shakes in the same way.

Cook's Notes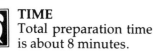

TIME
Total preparation time is about 8 minutes.

BUYING GUIDE
Malt extract is a dark brown, sticky syrup derived from barley. It is sold in health food stores.

WATCHPOINT
Return the remaining ice and ice cream to the freezer until needed, or they may melt.

●365 calories per drink

Cook's Notes

Midnight Noggin'

SERVES 4
2 large egg yolks
2 tablespoons sugar
3-4 tablespoons brandy, rum or
    sherry
2½ cups milk
freshly ground nutmeg, for dusting
    (optional)

1 Put the egg yolks and sugar into a large bowl and beat together, then gradually beat in the brandy.
2 Pour the milk into a small, heavy-bottomed saucepan and heat gently until almost boiling. Remove from the heat and slowly pour the hot

TIME
Preparation time is about 10 minutes.

SERVING IDEAS
This warming drink is an ideal night-cap. Sweeten the drinks with sugar.

?

DID YOU KNOW
Noggin is an old English word for a mug.

MICROWAVE
Follow step 1. In medium casserole, cook milk on Medium-high until very hot, stirring occasionally. Slowly blend milk into egg and brandy. Return to casserole. Cook on Medium-high until smooth and thickened, stirring very freqently.

●185 calories per portion

milk onto the egg and brandy mixture, stirring constantly.
3 Return the mixture to the rinsed-out pan and stir over very low heat for about 1 minute, until smooth and

very slightly thickened.
4 Strain immediately into 4 warmed mugs or heatproof tumblers. Sprinkle with nutmeg, if liked, and serve at once (see Serving Ideas).

233

Milky Snacks

SERVES 4
4 ripe bananas
4 eggs
4 teaspoons honey
juice of 2 small oranges
2½ cups milk
½ teaspoon ground cinnamon

1 Put the bananas, eggs and honey in a blender and work until smooth (see Cook's Tip).
2 Add the orange juice, milk and cinnamon and blend again.
3 Pour into 4 tall glasses and serve.

Cook's Notes

TIME
This nutritious snack-in-a-glass takes just 2-3 minutes to prepare.

VARIATIONS
Add 2-3 tablespoons smooth peanut butter, chocolate frosting, chocolate and hazelnut spread or malt extract to the mixture in step 1. Or, omit the orange juice and use 4 teaspoons instant coffee powder dissolved in a little hot water. You may also add a scoop of ice cream to each serving or a little sherry, rum or brandy. Instead of milk use buttermilk, skimmed milk or half milk and half yogurt.

DID YOU KNOW
As this drink is rich in protein and vitamins, it is ideal to serve when there is no time to cook a meal.

COOK'S TIP
Blend the mixture in 2 batches, if necessary.

●295 calories per portion

Old English Mulled Ale

MAKES ABOUT 10 CUPS
7½ cups brown ale
½ cup light brown sugar
3-inch cinnamon stick
½ teaspoon ground nutmeg
¼ teaspoon ground ginger
pinch of ground cloves
1 lemon, thinly sliced
1¼ cups medium-dry sherry
    (see Buying Guide)

1 Pour 2½ cups ale into a very large saucepan. Add the sugar and heat gently, stirring constantly, until the sugar has dissolved.
2 Add the spices and lemon slices, then bring the ale to a boil, lower the heat slightly and simmer for 5 minutes approximately.
3 Remove from the heat and stir in the remaining ale and the sherry. Using a slotted spoon, remove the cinnamon stick and discard. Serve at once, while still warm and foaming, in mugs or heatproof glasses.

Cook's Notes

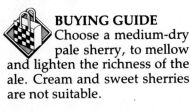

TIME
Total preparation and cooking time is 20-25 minutes approximately.

BUYING GUIDE
Choose a medium-dry pale sherry, to mellow and lighten the richness of the ale. Cream and sweet sherries are not suitable.

MICROWAVE
In large casserole, cook ale and sugar on High until hot. Stir to dissolve sugar. Cook on Medium-high until flavors blend. Follow step 3.

●115 calories per cup

Tropical Cocktails

Pina Colada
MAKES 6 LONG DRINKS
3 cups unsweetened pineapple
   juice
1¼ cups canned coconut cream or
   milk (see Buying Guide)
1½ cups white or golden rum
plenty of crushed ice, to serve

1 Quarter fill a glass pitcher with ice,
add one-third of the ingredients and
mix briskly. Alternatively, blend for
2-4 seconds in a blender.
2 Pour into 2 chilled glasses and
serve at once. Mix up 2 more batches
with the remaining ingredients.

Caribbean Blues
MAKES 6 SHORT DRINKS
1½ cups vodka
½ cup blue Curaçao
½ cup dry vermouth
plenty of crushed ice, to serve

1 Put all the ingredients, except the
ice, in a large glass pitcher and mix
very well.
2 Fill 6 chilled cocktail glasses with
crushed ice, pour the cocktail over
the ice and serve at once. Drink before the ice melts.

Planter's Punch
MAKES 6 LONG DRINKS
1½ cups dark rum
¾ cup lemon juice
4 teaspoons grenadine
1¼ cups orange juice
1¼ cups pineapple juice
few dashes of Angostura
   bitters
plenty of crushed ice,
   to serve

TO GARNISH
6 orange slices
6 lemon slices
6 cocktail cherries

1 Put all the ingredients, except the
ice, in a large glass pitcher and stir
very well.
2 Fill 6 large tumblers with crushed
ice and pour the punch over the ice.
Garnish each glass with an orange
and lemon slice and a cherry.

Cook's Notes

Piña Colada

 TIME
20 minutes preparation
in total.

BUYING GUIDE
Canned coconut cream
is available in large
supermarkets and health food
stores, but if it is difficult
to obtain, use a 6 oz block
creamed coconut and dissolve
it in 1¼ cups hot water.

● 365 calories per glass

Caribbean Blues

TIME
5-10 minutes prepar-
ation in total.

COOK'S TIP
To make crushed ice,
crush ice cubes in a
strong blender or in a food
processor. If you do not have
either, place the ice in a strong
plastic bag, squeeze out the air
and tie firmly. Place the bag on
a folded dish towel and beat
with a rolling pin.

● 160 calories per glass

Planter's Punch

TIME
5 minutes preparation
in total.

● 170 calories per glass

*Picture shows from left to right: Pina
Colada, Caribbean Blues and
Planter's Punch.*

Chestnut Cream Cake

MAKES 8-10 SLICES
1 x 18¼ oz supermoist vanilla
   cake mix
vegetable oil, for greasing
sugar, for coating

FILLING AND DECORATION
1 x 9 oz can chestnut spread
1¼ cups heavy cream
1 tablespoon brandy
candied chestnuts, sliced, to
   decorate

1 Preheat the oven to 350°. Lightly grease two 8-inch cake pans, then lightly coat the pans with sugar, tipping out the excess that remains (see Cook's Tip).

2 Divide the mixture evenly between prepared pans and spread evenly by gently tilting pans. Bake for 30-35 minutes, until the cakes are golden and springy to the touch.

3 Cool for 10 minutes, then turn out of the pans onto a wire rack. Leave the cakes to cool completely.

4 To serve, cut each cake in half horizontally with a long serrated knife. Whip the cream until standing in soft peaks, then fold in the chestnut spread and brandy. Use one third of the cream mixture to sandwich the cake layers together. Spread half the remaining cream mixture over the top and sides of the cake, so that they are coated.

5 Spoon remaining cream mixture into a pastry bag fitted with a star tip and pipe a decorative pattern on the top of the cake. Decorate with slices of candied chestnuts. Refrigerate until required.

Cook's Notes

TIME
Preparation (including baking and cooling) takes about 2 hours. Filling and decorating the cakes take about 20 minutes.

COOK'S TIP
Sugaring the cake pans makes it much easier to remove the baked cakes when they have cooled.

VARIATION
Use rum instead of brandy and maraschino cherries instead of sliced candied chestnuts.

● 360 calories per slice

Chocolate Button Cake

MAKES 8-10 SLICES
¾ cup all-purpose flour
2 tablespoons cocoa
1 cup sugar
2 eggs
⅔ cup milk
1 teaspoon vanilla
½ cup margarine, melted
shortening and flour, for greasing

FILLING AND TOPPING
2 cups confectioners' sugar
⅓ cup cocoa
3 tablespoons margarine, softened
about 3 tablespoons milk
1 teaspoon vanilla
candy-covered chocolate buttons

1 Preheat oven to 350°. Grease two 8-inch cake pans with shortening. Dust with flour. Tip out excess.
2 Sift the flour and cocoa into a large bowl. Stir in the sugar, then make a well in the center. Beat the eggs with the milk and vanilla, then add to the dry ingredients together with the margarine. Beat on low for 30 seconds, then increase the speed to high for 3 minutes.
3 Divide the mixture equally between the 2 prepared pans. Burst any large air bubbles with the point of a knife, then bake the cakes until springy to the touch.
4 Cool cakes in pans for 5 minutes. Turn out onto a rack to cool completely.
5 To make the filling and topping, sift the confectioners' sugar and cocoa into a bowl, then add the margarine, and cream together. Add 2 tablespoons milk and vanilla and beat. Add the remaining milk until a good spreading consistency.
6 Place 1 cake on a serving plate and spread with half the chocolate mixture. Place the other cake on top and spread with the remaining chocolate mixture. Arrange the candies on top. Leave for about 30 minutes, to firm, before cutting.

Cook's Notes

TIME
35-40 minutes preparation (including baking), plus cooling time for the cakes. Allow extra time for the filling and topping.

STORAGE
The finished cake will keep for about 4 days in an airtight container.

FOR CHILDREN
If the cake is to be the centerpiece of a children's party buffet, decorate the top of the cake with sugar flowers or colored sugar strands as well as the candy-covered chocolate buttons just before serving. Miniature toys make the cake more festive.

●510 calories per slice

Chocolate Peppermint Cake

MAKES 20 SLICES
4 oz (4 squares) semi-sweet
    chocolate
1¼ cups milk
1½ cups light brown sugar,
    firmly packed
½ lb tub margarine
2 eggs, separated
2 cups all-purpose flour
1 teaspoon bicarbonate of soda
shortening and extra flour, for
    greasing

FROSTING AND DECORATION
½ cup butter or margarine,
    softened
1½ cups confectioners' sugar, sifted
few drops of green food coloring
few drops of peppermint
    flavoring
2-3 tablespoons water
1 × 3½ oz package chocolate
    sprinkles
4 peppermint chocolate thins,
    cut diagonally in half
1 oz (1 square) semi-sweet
    chocolate, grated

1 Preheat the oven to 325°. Grease a 2-inch deep 8-inch square cake pan with shortening and lightly dust with the extra flour. Tip out the excess flour.
2 Break the chocolate into a small bowl set over a pan of simmering water. Add half the milk and half the sugar. When the chocolate has melted, remove from the heat and gently stir in the remaining milk and mix well (see Watchpoint).
3 Beat the fat and remaining sugar in a bowl with the egg yolks. Beat in the chocolate mixture, then sift in the flour and bicarbonate of soda. Mix until well blended, then beat for 1 minute.
4 In a clean dry bowl, beat the egg whites until standing in stiff peaks. Then, using a large metal spoon, carefully fold 1 tablespoon into the mixture, then fold the rest of the egg whites into the chocolate mixture.
5 Turn mixture into prepared pan and smooth the top with a spatula. Bake in the oven for 1-1¼ hours, until the cake springs back when lightly pressed. Turn onto a wire rack the right way up and leave to cool completely.
6 Meanwhile, to make peppermint frosting, beat butter until it is soft and creamy. Gradually beat in the confectioners' sugar, green coloring, peppermint flavoring and enough water to give a smooth buttercream which will hold its shape.
7 Spread one-third of the frosting around the sides of the cake. Spread the chocolate sprinkles out on a piece of wax paper then, holding the cake firmly in both hands, dip it in the sprinkles until the sides are completely coated.
8 Put the cake on a serving plate. Spread half the remaining frosting over the top of the cake then, using a

pastry bag with a large rosette tip, pipe the rest in a border around the edge of the cake. Arrange the peppermint chocolate halves in the piped frosting, then sprinkle the grated chocolate over the center of the cake.

Cook's Notes

TIME
The cake takes about 30 minutes to prepare, 1-1¼ hours to bake and about 30 minutes to finish.

WATCHPOINT
Do not stir until the chocolate has almost melted or it may become granular and spoil the result.

●280 calories per slice

Crispy Peach Cake

MAKES 6-8 SLICES
1 cup crisp rice cereal
6 tablespoons margarine
1 cup marshmallows
1 cup pieces of plain toffee candy
shortening, for greasing

FILLING
½ tablespoon powdered unflavored
   gelatin
3 tablespoons water
2½ cups cold milk
2 × 2½ oz packets butterscotch
   pudding mix
2 small bananas
1 teaspoon lemon juice
1 × 8¼ oz can peach slices, drained

1 Oil a 8-inch springform cake pan.
Put rice cereal into a large bowl.
2 Put the margarine, marshmallows
and toffee candy into a heavy-
bottomed pan. Heat gently, stirring
occasionally, until melted, then beat
until smooth. Pour onto rice cereal
and mix until evenly blended.
3 Press the cereal mixture evenly
over the base and sides of the prepared pan. Leave in a cool place for
at least 2 hours to firm.
4 Sprinkle the gelatin over the water
in a small heatproof bowl. Leave to
soak for 5 minutes, then stand bowl
in a pan of gently simmering water
for 1-2 minutes, stirring occasionally, until the gelatin has dissolved.
Remove bowl from pan.
5 Pour the milk into a large bowl and
beat in butterscotch mixes. Leave
until thickened, then fold in gelatin.
6 Slice the bananas, then cut each
slice across into 3 strips. Toss in
lemon juice, then fold into butterscotch mixture. Refrigerate for 1
hour, or until on point of setting.
7 Carefully remove cereal shell from
pan and place on a serving plate.
Turn butterscotch mixture into shell
and level the surface. Leave in a cool
place for about 1 hour, until set.
Arrange the peach slices and serve.

Cook's Notes

TIME
45 minutes prepara-
tion, plus 2 hours for
the shell to firm and a further 2
hours for the filling to set.

WATCHPOINT
Do not assemble the
cake more than 1
hour before serving or the
crispy shell will become too
soft and spoil the taste.

SERVING IDEAS
This cake is ideal for a
birthday party. Tie a
ribbon around the sides for a
more festive look.

●490 calories per slice

Heavenly Slices

MAKES 6 SLICES
1 oblong layer cake, about
6½ × 2 inches
5 tablespoons strawberry jelly
½ cup toasted slivered almonds
½ cup strawberry-flavored fondant
frosting (see Buying Guide)
silver balls to finish
confectioners' sugar, for dusting

1 Strain the jelly into a small saucepan. Heat gently, stirring constantly, until runny. Remove the pan from the heat.

2 Brush sides of the cake evenly with two-thirds of the jelly, then coat with the almonds (see Preparation). Brush the top with most of the remaining jelly.

3 Sift an even layer of confectioners' sugar over the work surface, then roll out fondant to a 8 × 3-inch rectangle. With a sharp small knife, trim fondant to fit top of cake. (Reserve the trimmings to make the flower decorations.)

4 Lift the fondant on the rolling pin and lay it on top of the cake. Press gently in place, then flute the edges or smooth them against the sides of the cake to neaten. (Fluting the edges with your finger and thumb will give the most attractive finish.)

5 Knead the fondant trimmings together. Dust the counter top with confectioners' sugar again, then roll out the fondant and cut into as many circles as possible, using a 1-inch (petits fours) fluted cookie cutter.

6 Mold the sides of each with your fingers to make flower shapes, then press a silver ball into the center of each one. Arrange the flowers on the top of the cake, securing them in position with a little jelly.

7 Transfer the cake to a serving plate. Cut across into slices with a long, serrated knife.

Cook's Notes

TIME
Preparation time is about 35 minutes.

BUYING GUIDE
Fondant frosting is sold in most large supermarkets. There are several varieties, each colored to match the flavor. Store in a cool place for up to 2 years.

PREPARATION
To coat the cake sides.

Spread the almonds in a thick strip on wax paper. Hold top and bottom of cake between the palms of your hands, then press each jelly-covered side firmly into the nuts. Place cake right way up and fill in any gaps in the coating by hand.

●135 calories per slice

Rose Marble Ring

MAKES 12 SLICES
¾ cup butter, softened
¼ cup shortening
1 cup sugar
5 eggs
2¼ cups all-purpose flour
4 teaspoons baking powder
1 teaspoon salt
2 tablespoons rose water (see
    Buying Guide)
few drops of red food coloring
½ teaspoon vanilla
melted shortening, for
    greasing

FROSTING
1 cup confectioners' sugar, sifted
1 tablespoon rose water
1-2 tablespoons water
candied rose petals, to decorate
    (see Buying Guide)

1 Preheat the oven to 350°. Generously grease a 12-cup Bundt pan.
2 Cream the butter with the shortening. Add the sugar and continue creaming until light and fluffy. Add the eggs, one at a time, beating well after each addition. Scrape down the side of the bowl as necessary. Sift the flour, baking powder and salt over the batter, then stir in.
3 Turn half the mixture into a separate bowl. Stir the rose water into one half and tint pink with a few drops of food coloring. Stir the vanilla into the other half.
4 Place alternate spoonfuls of the 2 mixtures in the Bundt pan. Draw the blade of a knife through the mixture, first one way and then the other. Level the surface of the mixture carefully, taking care not to mix the colors too much. Bake in the oven for about 45 minutes, until a fine warmed skewer inserted in the center comes out clean.
5 Let the cake stand in the pan for 3 minutes, then turn out on a wire rack. Leave to cool completely.
6 To make the frosting, blend the

Cook's Notes

TIME
The cake takes about 1 hour to make and bake. Allow about 1 hour for cooling, and 5-10 minutes for frosting, plus setting time.

BUYING GUIDE
You can buy rose water and candied rose petals from delicatessens and gourmet stores.

WATCHPOINT
Take care to grease the pan well so that the baked cake will turn out easily, without breaking.

● 340 calories per slice

confectioners' sugar with the rose water and gradually add enough water to give a smooth, runny consistency. Spoon the frosting over the top and let it trickle down the sides. Scatter a few candied rose petals over the top and leave to set. Transfer to a serving plate.

Sherry Layer Cake

MAKES 10-12 SLICES
1½ cups all-purpose flour
1½ teaspoons baking powder
¼ teaspoon salt
½ cup butter, softened
½ cup shortening
1 cup sugar
1 tablespoon grated orange rind
2 eggs
⅔ cup milk
2 tablespoons sweet sherry
2 tablespoons orange juice
shortening for greasing

SHERRY BUTTER FROSTING
6 tablespoons butter, softened
2 cups confectioners' sugar, sifted
2 tablespoons sweet sherry
frosted flowers (see Preparation)

1 Preheat the oven to 350°. Grease and lightly flour two 8-inch cake pans. Tip out the excess flour.
2 Combine the flour, baking powder and salt in a sifter and set aside.

Beat the butter and shortening until creamy, then gradually add the sugar and orange rind. Beat in the eggs, one at a time. Add the milk on low speed. Sift the flour mixture over the batter and stir in by hand.
3 Divide the mixture between the prepared pans and level each surface. Stand the pans on a cookie sheet, then bake in the oven for 25-30 minutes or until the cakes are springy to the touch.
4 Cool the cakes for 1-2 minutes, then turn out of the pans. Place the cakes, the right way up, on a wire rack and leave to cool completely.
5 To make the frosting, beat the butter until very soft, then slowly beat in the confectioners' sugar. Beat until the mixture is pale and creamy, then beat in the sherry.
6 To assemble the cake, place 1 cake on a serving plate. Mix together the sherry and orange juice and spoon half evenly over the cake. Spread one-third of the frosting over the cake, then top with the second cake. Sprinkle with the remaining sherry and orange mixture. Spread top with half of remaining frosting, leaving a ¼-inch border. Mark a

Cook's Notes

TIME
10 minutes preparation and 25-30 minutes baking. Cooling takes about 1 hour. Assembling and decorating takes 20 minutes.

PREPARATION
Choose small, non-poisonous and colorful fresh flowers. Wash and dry the flowers, then brush with slightly beaten egg white. Sprinkle with superfine sugar and leave 15 minutes to dry. The flowers are not intended to be eaten.

●460 calories per portion

wavy pattern with a small spatula.
7 Place remaining frosting in a pastry bag fitted with a small star tip and pipe a border of small rosettes around top edge of cake. Refrigerate for 20-25 minutes to firm. Decorate with frosted flowers.

Spinning Top Cake

MAKES 16 SLICES
2 cups all-purpose flour
2 teaspoons baking powder
1 cup margarine, softened
1 cup sugar
4 eggs
few drops of red food coloring
shortening and flour, for greasing

FROSTING
1¼ cups butter, softened
5 cups confectioners' sugar, sifted
2 tablespoons shredded coconut
few drops each of red, green and
**   yellow food coloring**

1 Preheat the oven to 350°.
2 Fully grease two 8-inch cake pans with shortening. Dust with flour, then tip out the excess flour.
3 Sift flour and baking powder into a large bowl, add the margarine, sugar and eggs, then beat for approximately 1 minute.
4 Spoon half the batter into the cake pans. Tint the remaining batter pink with a few drops of red food coloring. Add the pink batter to the cake pans so they are filled with alternating pink and white batter.
5 Bake in oven for 30-35 minutes or until the cakes golden brown and springy to the touch.
6 Turn the cakes out onto a wire rack and leave to cool completely.
7 To make frostings, put the butter into a bowl and beat in the confectioners' sugar a little at a time. Use a small amount of frosting to fill the two cakes. Place one-third of the remaining frosting in a bowl and thin with a little warm water and spread around the sides of the cake.
8 Spread out the coconut on a piece of wax paper. Hold the top and bottom of the cake firmly between both hands and then roll sides of the cake in the coconut until evenly coated. Place the cake on a serving plate.
9 Put 4 tablespoons of frosting in a separate bowl and add a few drops of red coloring. Repeat with green coloring and combine some red and yellow coloring to make orange. Leave the rest of the frosting plain.
10 Mark the cake into 8 sections and rough ice in different colors. Pipe plain frosting around top and base. Serve on day it is frosted.

Cook's Notes

TIME
30 minutes preparation and 30-35 minutes cooking, plus cooling. Frosting the cake takes about 20 minutes in all.

VARIATION
Instead of a rough frosting for the top of the cake, pipe rosettes of different-colored frosting.

●475 calories per slice

Blackberry Deep Dish Pie

SERVES 4-6
½ package (about 1⅓ cups)
   pie crust mix
water, for mixing
vanilla ice cream, to serve

FILLING
1 quart blackberries (see
   Cook's Tips)
6 cups pared, cored and sliced
   tart apples
1½ cups sugar
½ cup all-purpose flour
1 teaspoon allspice
2 tablespoons butter
1 tablespoon lemon juice

1 Preheat the oven to 425°.
2 Prepare the pie crust dough according to the package directions. Wrap in plastic wrap and chill for at least 30 minutes.
3 Meanwhile, to prepare the filling, place the blackberries and apples into a large bowl. Combine the sugar, flour and spices, then mix gently with the fruit.
4 Pour the mixture into a 1½-quart baking dish. Dot the filling with butter and sprinkle with lemon juice.
5 On a lightly floured surface, roll out the dough to a circle 1-inch larger than the top of the dish. Cover the fruit and tuck the edges inside the bowl, then crimp to seal. Cut a couple of slits in the center.
6 Place the dish on a cookie sheet to catch any drips while cooking and bake for 1 hour. Serve hot.

Cook's Notes

TIME
45 minutes preparation and 1 hour cooking.

COOK'S TIPS
Frozen blackberries, if available, do not have to be thawed before being added to this dessert.
   Use other soft fruits such as raspberries or blueberries.

SERVING IDEAS
This pie can also be served with custard or a different flavored ice cream.

●745 calories per portion

Blackberry Bars

MAKES 16 SLICES
½ cup margarine
½ cup sugar
¼ cup maple syrup
1 egg, beaten
2 cups all-purpose flour
1 teaspoon baking powder
1 teaspoon cinnamon
½ cup blackberry jam
½ cup finely chopped walnuts
shortening and flour, for greasing

1 Preheat the oven to 350°. Lightly grease and flour a 11½ × 7½ × ½-inch aluminum foil pan. Shake out the excess flour.
2 Beat the margarine and sugar until pale and fluffy. Add the syrup and egg, a little at a time, beating thoroughly. Scrape down the sides of the bowl, if necessary, while beating the mixture.
3 Sift the flour, baking powder and cinnamon together, then beat into the creamed syrup and egg mixture in 3 batches.
4 Spread two-thirds of the mixture into the prepared pan. Spread the jam over, then spoon remaining mixture on top and spread it as evenly as possible with the back of the spoon (see Cook's Tip). Sprinkle over the walnuts and bake just above center of the oven for about 35-40 minutes, until golden.
5 Leave to cool in the pan, then cut into 16 slices.

Cook's Notes

TIME
Preparation takes about 10 minutes and cooking 35-40 minutes. Allow extra time for cooling.

STORAGE
Store the spiced bars in an airtight container and eat within 2-3 days of baking the bars.

COOK'S TIP
Spooning the mixture into the pan and then spreading it helps prevent it mixing in with the jam. It is not necessary to completely cover the jam because the mixture will spread enough during cooking.

● 210 calories per slice

Blackberry Cheesecake

MAKES 6-8 SLICES
2 cups graham cracker crumbs
4 tablespoons butter, melted

FILLING AND TOPPING
1 lb cottage cheese
1 x 6 oz carton plain yogurt
2 eggs, separated
grated rind of 1 orange
4-6 tablespoons sugar
4 teaspoons unflavored gelatin
¼ cup water
2 teaspoons cornstarch
1 lb canned blackberries
**   drained, with syrup reserved**

1 Mix the crumbs with the melted butter, then press evenly over the base of a deep loose-bottomed 8-inch springform cake pan. Cover and refrigerate.

2 To make the filling, beat the cheese with a wooden spoon until soft. Gradually beat in the yogurt, egg yolks, orange rind and sugar.

3 Sprinkle the gelatin over the water in a small, heatproof bowl. Leave to soak for 5 minutes, until spongy, then stand the bowl in a pan of gently simmering water for 1-2 minutes, stirring occasionally, until the gelatin has dissolved.

4 Remove the bowl from the pan and allow the gelatin to cool slightly. Beat the gelatin into the cheese mixture. Cover and refrigerate until the mixture is on the point of setting.

5 In a clean, dry bowl, beat the egg whites until standing in soft peaks, then fold into the cheese mixture with a large metal spoon. Turn into the prepared pan, cover and refrigerate for about 2 hours, until set.

6 Meanwhile, to make the topping, in a small pan, blend the cornstarch with a little of the blackberry syrup. Gradually blend in the remaining syrup. Bring slowly to a boil, stirring constantly, and cook for 1-2 minutes, until smooth and thickened. Remove from the heat, stir in the blackberries and leave to cool.

7 To serve, run a spatula around the side of the cheesecake, then carefully remove the sides of the pan. Place the cake on a serving plate and spread the blackberry mixture over the top. Serve chilled.

Cook's Notes

TIME
45 minutes preparation, plus chilling and setting time.

●500 calories per slice

Blackberry Marble

SERVES 6
1 × 3 oz package
   blackberry-flavored gelatin
1 cup boiling water
1 cup cold water
½ cup heavy cream
½ cup plain yogurt

1 Dissolve the gelatin in the boiling water, stirring until dissolved, about 2 minutes. Stir in the cold water.

2 Chill until just about set.
3 Whip the cream until soft peaks form. Put half the blackberry gelatin into a large bowl, then fold in the cream with a large metal spoon. Beat the yogurt into the remaining gelatin.
4 Cover each mixture and place in the refrigerator 5-10 minutes, until on the point of setting.
5 Lightly fold the blackberry and yogurt mixture through the creamy blackberry mixture to give a marbled effect. Cover and refrigerate for a maximum of 8 hours, until set.
6 To serve, scoop into individual glass bowls. Serve chilled.

Cook's Notes

TIME
25 minutes preparation, plus setting time.

COOK'S TIP
Combining yogurt with the cream makes this a light dessert. For a special dinner party dessert, use all heavy cream and omit the plain yogurt.

● 240 calories per portion

Blackberry Sponge

SERVES 4
1 tablespoon cornstarch
3 tablespoons sugar
1 cup water
1 tart apple, pared, quartered,
  cored and finely chopped
1 cup blackberries
margarine or butter, for greasing

SPONGE TOPPING
2 eggs, separated
¼ cup sugar
½ cup all-purpose flour
confectioners' sugar, for
  dredging

1 Preheat the oven to 375°. Grease a 1-quart baking dish.
2 Mix the cornstarch with the sugar, then blend to a smooth paste with a little of the water.

3 Pour the remaining water into a small saucepan, add the apples and simmer for 5-8 minutes, until tender. Stir the cornstarch mixture, then add to the pan together with the blackberries. Simmer, stirring, for about 5 minutes, until the mixture thickens.
4 Turn the mixture into the prepared dish and place in the oven while you prepare the topping (see Cook's Tip).
5 In a clean, dry bowl, beat the egg whites until standing in stiff peaks. Add 1 tablespoon of the sugar and beat until stiff again. Add half the remaining sugar and 1 egg yolk and beat until creamy. Add the rest of the sugar and remaining egg yolk and beat in thoroughly. Sift in the flour, then fold it in with a large metal spoon.
6 Remove the dish from the oven. Quickly pour the sponge mixture over the top, then spread it evenly to cover the fruit completely. Return the dish to the oven and bake for a

Cook's Notes

TIME
Preparation and baking take about 1 hour.

COOK'S TIP
The topping cooks more quickly when spread over a hot fruit base.

SERVING IDEAS
This dessert can be served hot with custard or vanilla ice cream, or cold with plain yogurt.

● 210 calories per portion

further 25-30 minutes, until the topping is golden brown and firm to the touch.
7 Sift confectioners' sugar generously over the pudding. Serve hot or cold (see Serving Ideas).

Blackberry Summer Pudding

SERVES 4

1⅔ cups blackberries
1½ cups mixed blackcurrants and
  red currants, stripped from
  their stems
½ cup sugar
1 tablespoon orange juice
5-7 thin slices day-old white bread,
  with crusts removed

1 Put the mixed currants into a
heavy-bottomed saucepan. Add the
sugar and orange juice and bring
slowly to a boil. Cover and cook very
gently for about 5 minutes, stirring
occasionally, until the currants are
tender and the juices are flowing.
2 Add the blackberries and cook
gently for 2-3 minutes. Remove from
the heat and leave to cool.
3 Meanwhile, use most of the bread
to line the base and sides of a 2½-
cup baking bowl or pudding mold.

Cut the bread so that it fits neatly
and use the trimmings to fill any
gaps completely.
4 Put 5 tablespoons of the fruit
juices and 2 tablespoons of fruit into
separate small containers, cover and
reserve in the refrigerator. Spoon
the remaining fruits and juices into
the bread-lined bowl and cover completely with the remaining bread.
5 Put a small plate or lid which fits

just inside the rim of the bowl on top
of the pudding. Weight the plate
down, then leave the pudding in the
refrigerator overnight.
6 To serve, run a round-bladed
knife around the top edge of the
pudding to loosen it, then turn it out
onto a serving plate. Spoon the reserved fruit juices over any areas of
bread that are not colored and pile
the reserved fruit on top.

Cook's Notes

TIME
30 minutes preparation,
plus at least 8 hours
chilling.

WATCHPOINTS
Do not overcook the
fruits; they should be
tender but not mushy.
  Make sure that there are no
gaps in the bread casing, or the
pudding will not hold its shape
well when it is turned out.

STORAGE
Prepare the pudding
up to the end of step 5
and store in the refrigerator for
up to 48 hours.

SERVING IDEAS
Lightly whipped cream
is the traditional
accompaniment to serve with
this refreshing dessert.

●215 calories per portion

Blackberry Treat

SERVES 6
1 quart soft scoop vanilla
ice cream
1½ lb frozen blackberries (see
Variations)
⅔ cup sugar
4 tablespoons blackberry jelly

1 Put the ice cream into a 1½-quart freezerproof serving dish. Using a large metal spoon, press the ice cream over the base of the dish, then level the surface. Cover with aluminum foil and freeze until it is required.
2 Place the blackberries in a large bowl. Sprinkle over the sugar and mix gently, then leave at room temperature for about 2 hours, turn-

ing the fruit occasionally, until the berries are just thawed.
3 Drain the sugared blackberries thoroughly, reserving ¼ cup of the syrup. Uncover the ice cream and spread the berries evenly over the top. Cover the dish and return it to the freezer while making the glaze.
4 Put the jelly and reserved syrup

into a small heavy-bottomed sauce-pan. Stir over low heat until the jelly has melted, then allow the blackberry jelly glaze to cool for about 2-3 minutes.
5 Uncover the dish and pour the cooled glaze evenly over the black-berries. Serve the dessert at once, straight from the dish.

Cook's Notes

 TIME
2 hours preparation then 10-15 minutes.

VARIATIONS
Use fresh blackberries when they are in season. Sprinkle with the sugar, then cover and refriger-ate for 1 hour, until well chilled and a syrup has formed. Use raspberries or strawberries in-stead of blackberries and seed-less raspberry jam in place of the blackberry jelly.

! WATCHPOINT
Do not let the berries soften too much, or they will lose their shape.

●440 calories per portion